Managing On Purpose:

A Framework for Guiding Success in the Workplace

JAMES P. HALL

ISBN: 1467916005
ISBN-13: 978-1467916004

For Tim Berney
Best wishes
[signature] 1/26/12

DEDICATION

For Marsha

CONTENTS

FOREWORD

In the thick of a battle, you wouldn't expect to see a general teaching majors or colonels how to communicate better with their men. You wouldn't expect to see the general working with them on other aspects of their jobs such as administration and discipline. We could say the same things about the majors and the colonels: they won't be working with their lieutenants on the same kinds of topics while a battle rages around them.

After the Army of Northern Virginia was defeated at Gettysburg, General Robert E. Lee reflected that if he'd had General Stonewall Jackson with him at Gettysburg, he might have won. Jackson had been killed shortly before that battle. Without Jackson, Lee, whose style was to give his generals considerable latitude in carrying out what were usually general battle plans, lacked the number and caliber of leaders like Jackson, officers who had the overall "skill set" that had proven so valuable in earlier encounters with the enemy.

But as Secretary of Defense Donald Rumsfeld somewhat infamously said early in the war in Iraq, you go to war with the army you have, not with the army you want—and this would have been true of Lee at Gettysburg.

Armies and organizations face this same leadership and management issue every day. They go to battle, as it were, with the armies they have, and they recognize that there is a standard of leader/manager that they'd like to have in place, but in many cases they find themselves making do with considerably less. Lee went into battle at Gettysburg with generals like Longstreet, Hill, Ewell, Pickett and Stuart, certainly worthy and tested officers, but none of whom possessed the aggregate qualifications of a Stonewall Jackson.

As we think about developing the leaders/managers we need in the modern workplace, we confront two issues. The first is that the battle, as it were, has already started. We can't call it off, saying, "Oops! We're not ready!" The second is that the people we have throughout our leader/manager ranks are all over the place when it comes to the kind of preparation they've had and the qualifications they possess.

You might say, perhaps, that this shouldn't be. Don't we have the wherewithal to prepare managers? It appears that we do. We have entire academic departments in place, producing thousands of management majors every year. We have professional management associations doing cutting edge research. We have management development programs available for general use, and many organizations have in-house departments creating company-specific development programs for their managers and supervisors. Not insignificantly, we also have the school of hard knocks. Some occupy leadership positions with little formal preparation; they have learned on the job. Finally, there is a management development workshop or seminar coming to your town this very weekend.

Even though the large and vibrant discipline of management development is in place, I still believe we confront the two issues identified above: the battle has started, and the people we have in place possess widely varying qualifications to fight it.

Now, I am foolish if I think the slender volume you hold in your hands at this moment is going to address both of these issues to our complete satisfaction. I was born at night, as the saying goes, but not *last* night. My goal for this book is very modest. That goal is that it provide a place to start. As I've worked in organizations of all sizes, I've often wished for a way to establish a common set of understandings among the management team. I've wished that it were possible to have conversations with members of that team about the core topics that they really need to know about—if they are to go about their jobs as successfully as they can, and if they are to keep the organization from getting into trouble of various kinds should they (the management team) do things the wrong way.

My goal for this book is that it be that kind of foundational, "threshold" program. I want it to be the one song in the hymnal that every member of the congregation knows by heart.

I don't minimize the difficulty of the job at hand. I admire Dr. Scott Peck's classic book *The Road Less Traveled*.[1] The book has a famous first sentence: "Life is difficult." Dr. Peck asserts in the book that thinking that life *isn't* difficult can lead to problems. Because many think life should be easy, they never develop the wherewithal to recognize and solve the problems that inevitably come to each of us. So he wants to make that point right away: life is difficult.

Management is difficult. We can define management as the application of specific knowledge, skill and ability, directed toward the achievement of organization goals—often through the efforts of other people. Management requires knowledge, patience, intelligence, empathy, courage, flexibility, skill, communication—the list could go on. However each of us arrives in a management position (and the paths to management positions are many), few of us have mastered all of its dimensions and complexities easily.

Management is difficult indeed. As I say, my modest goal with this book is simply to provide a starting place, a line in the sand, so to speak, from which we can begin.

Managing on Purpose can of course simply be read as a book on management, or it can comprise a series of training sessions that you conduct with everyone in your organization who has manager/supervisor responsibility. These sessions will put a range of managers' duties and responsibilities on the table for them to consider and discuss. After such initial training, all managers would not only be singing from the same page of the company hymnal, they would also have the awareness they need to succeed in the many dimensions of their jobs. We won't let them fall into any ruts or potholes. They won't be able to say, should some later catastrophe befall them, "I wish someone would have told me about this!"

Managing on Purpose provides the content and methodology for this training. In addition to delivering essential content, each of its eighteen chapters includes a section called For Further Consideration, which contains questions that provide the opportunity for broader and deeper inquiry into the topic at hand. It requires participants to apply concepts they've just read about to their specific, on-the-job situations.

I take this approach because of my experience with other training programs, and because of my knowledge of how precious time is in the workplace. Once again, excellent programs are out there, but even one component of them (a unit on team building for example) can take hours or days to complete. Organizations rarely have that kind of time, nor are they often willing to incur the related expense. The book you're holding consists of short chapters which can be read in less than half-an-hour. These chapters are accompanied by the "Consideration" questions just mentioned, and the reading and discussion needed to understand and apply the lessons of a given chapter can occur in 60-90 minutes. My thought is that organizations may want to cover different chapters in "brown bag" lunch sessions with their supervisors and managers.

The first audience I envision for the book consists of decision makers who are charged with preparing leaders and managers in their organizations. If this is you, you can proceed through the material in the book on your own, or arrange a series of instructor led or online sessions. Once you've familiarized yourself with the content, you can arrange for its delivery to all those in your organization with management responsibility. The book can thus comprise the basic (perhaps the first) management training program that you ask all of your people to complete. Later you can add more detailed, complex, and organization-specific lessons for your people, either individually or collectively as needed.

The second audience I envision consists of foremen, leads, first line supervisors, department managers, owners/managers of your own businesses, occupants of the C Suite, managers of convenience stores, teachers, principals, farmers, and pastors—all those who have management or supervisory responsibility. As I suggested earlier, you may have received your current working assignment without being told its full scope, nor being told how to address each of the dimensions of your job you now face. We address many of these areas in the pages that follow.

Over the years I've come to believe that most managers do have the potential to be successful—to elicit optimum results from people, materials and processes toward the achievement of organization goals. In some cases, we simply haven't been told how. Regardless, starting now, we can all be more effective than we've been. And once again, what I mean by "effective" is the degree to which our efforts approach the "optimization" standard—the degree to which we optimize (get the most from) the human effort, material quality and process capability entrusted to us.

My ideas as to how we can move the bar higher are embedded in the title of the book. The first part, *Managing on Purpose*, suggests that managers should be purposeful. In a complex, difficult working environment, someone needs to have his/her hands on the controls. Within each of our respective workplaces, it should be clear to everyone what the working agenda is moment-to-moment, and what everyone's responsibilities are in terms of the items on the agenda. We need to manage on purpose.

My subtitle is *A Framework for Guiding Success in the Workplace*. Managers can lack a meaningful framework, a construct—an idea or paradigm—of what's expected of them. Sometimes it's hard for them to see the big picture. This can be a forest and trees situation. In the workplace, sometimes particular trees keep managers from seeing other things out there in the forest. If they can't "see" the full picture of all they need to know and what they need to do, it's difficult for them to be successful—they are in a sense flying blind (which is dangerous when flying through a forest). In later chapters we provide a framework that will get managers out from behind particular trees, safely into and through that forest on the other side.

One thing you'll discover is that there's a great deal *in* the management framework. This means that there is a great deal for managers to know (they need a lot of information); for them to know how to do (they need a lot of skill); and for them to be (they need to be in fact many people, housed in one body).

When people talk about this they talk in terms of managers wearing many hats, and of things falling through the cracks. This "hats" idea isn't productive, primarily because it suggests that manager success is as simple as doffing one hat and donning another. It isn't. Management, remember, is difficult. Rather than the donning and doffing of hats, managers must call on a variety of genuine, "hardwired" inner resources to deal successfully with all they encounter in the workplace: people, interdepartmental relationships, technical issues, policies, regulations, quality, and so on.

The framework of the management job that we develop needs to both identify the many dimensions of a manager's job and then assign priorities to them. This lessens the likelihood of something falling through a crack (do any of our floors, speaking of this, really have cracks in them?). A great many things "come at" managers, sometimes all at once, and we need to help them identify, prioritize and respond to these things—what I will call "inputs." We need to assist managers in prioritizing or "filtering" these inputs.

A key word in my subtitle is "Guiding." Throughout, I emphasize the concept of purpose, of "intentionality." Things should happen in the workplace because they're caused, planned for, proactively anticipated. Managers can't simply arrive at the workplace in the morning, unlock the door, and hope for the best. Any supervisor or manager, when asked, should be able to say immediately what he or she is doing at any given moment in time: what he or she *intends to do* to achieve a positive result. The latter is what the word "Success" means in the subtitle—achieving a positive result.

The first part of *Managing on Purpose*, comprised of Chapters One through Six, is called "Aspects." As its name suggests, this part looks at six aspects or facets of management: Purpose, Status, Value, Dimensions, Experience and Priorities. These establish the foundation of what management is and what it has been in our immediate past.

The second part of the book is called "Applications." In these twelve chapters, we consider the many ways in which management knowledge, skill and ability must be applied: to the concept of change, to people, to money, to planning, to compliance, to technology, to risk, and so on. Maybe we've become too casual about management as a skill and as a profession (given the multiple ways that people come to occupy management positions). If we have, we need to become more serious and systematic about it, recognizing it for the complex and valuable function that it can be in our organizations.

James P. Hall
Hanover, Pennsylvania
Fall 2011

Notes

1. Peck, Scott. *The Road Less Traveled*. New York: Touchstone, 2003. Print.

PART I:ASPECTS

1 THE NEED FOR PURPOSEFUL MANAGEMENT

Purpose in Organizations

My daughter and I had come to the big box store to buy a gift—a watch for my wife. We found the jewelry department and spent some time looking at the various options. While we looked, a sales associate stood by the cash register some fifteen feet or so from where we were, talking on her cell phone. After a few minutes, we saw two watches that we thought looked nice, and wanted to see them up close.

We tried to get the attention of the young woman talking on her phone, shuffling our feet, clearing our throats and trying to make eye contact. No luck. We tried for a few more minutes; as I recall, we may have even drummed our fingers or our keys on the counter. Nothing.

Finally, the young woman apparently realized that we weren't going away, put her hand with the phone down by her side, looked at us icily and said, "Do you *want* something?!" Not any more we didn't. We took our business elsewhere.

The jewelry department in the big box store exists to sell jewelry. A sales associate's purpose is to assist customers in buying that jewelry. In fact, the associate is to *facilitate* the buying of jewelry—in our case she was supposed to help us find what we wanted, and perhaps even sell us more than we'd come into the store to buy.

The big box store itself of course exists for a purpose: to provide in one large, convenient location a place where people can buy a variety of things they want and need. Within the store, people performing various functions work to facilitate this one main goal: to sell as many goods as possible to the greatest number of people at the highest profit margin possible.

The store, every store, every congregation of human beings, is or ought to be *purposeful*. In our example, people working in the big box store are there to carry out its purpose. People are grouped by department (e.g. clothing and sporting goods) and function (accounting and purchasing) to carry out the store's function efficiently.

Bees and ants seem to have this purpose and function thing down pretty well. From upper management through the worker ranks, assignments are clear and functions get performed (perhaps the absence of cell phones is key in this regard). However they're managing this, I don't think you'd ever hear a worker bee or ant say—except perhaps to the grasshopper who inadvertently lands on the hill or flies into the hive) "Do you *want* something?!" Everyone seems to have his or her role in the hive or hill down pat. They know what they're supposed to do, and they do it.

We human beings as managers and sales people apparently still have some work to do.

Preparing Associates

The interaction my daughter and I had with the sales associate in the jewelry department represents a major failure for the store. Remember, its primary reason for existing—selling goods for a profit—was not realized. Let's call our sales associate Sarah. What Sarah did was not only lose the sale, but she may have put at risk all future business my family and I might have with the store.

Let's name the big box store Caremart. For my daughter and me, Sarah was the face, brain, heart, hands and feet of Caremart: to us, she *was* Caremart. This is not a trivial point, this hands and feet business. The goal of upper management in any organization, way high up in the C Suite, is to translate its vision and mission into the concrete actions of everyone else in the organization. The degree to which that translation succeeds (in "informing" the actions of every associate) is the degree to which the organization ultimately succeeds.

In our example, let's be clear that the company itself isn't the sole cause of the difficulty we had. Sarah as a person shares some blame in Caremart's loss of all future Hall family business. Perhaps a company can't guarantee that *every* second an employee spends on the job will be purposeful and productive. However, even with no training, no preparation at all for how she was supposed to handle her job, Sarah could have handled the situation better than she did. In other words, Sarah the person shares some of the blame for Sarah the Caremart associate's bad performance.

There are others at whose feet we can lay blame. What about those of Sarah's manager?—her direct supervisor? Let's name Sarah's manager Esther. Esther is Jewelry Department Manager for Caremart, Anytown USA. Is Esther somehow the cause of Sarah's poor performance?

While other training specialists may have played a role in preparing Sarah for her job, Sarah does work for Esther. Sarah, once she steps behind the jewelry counter, is Esther's responsibility (with the caveat we made above about Sarah having to assume at least some personal responsibility). That said, isn't the primary failure here largely Esther's? Just as America's schools are to leave no child behind, we would think that Caremart the company strives to leave no sales associate behind—when it comes to preparing him or her to work productively in the store. As Sarah's direct supervisor, Esther is the Caremart agent who's supposed to make that happen.

But something obviously went wrong. To my daughter and me, Sarah was clearly the sales associate left behind.

Manager Responsibility

Here's another question. Where *was* Esther when our unfortunate interaction with Sarah occurred? As Sarah talked on the phone, she showed little evidence that she cared if we or anyone else heard what she was saying. She didn't appear to care, in other words, whether or not she was going to get caught misusing company time. Esther had apparently failed to instill in Sarah the importance of seeing to customer needs the *moment* the customer appears at the jewelry counter.

Where was Esther?? She may have been on a break. She may have been working with inventory. She may have been helping other customers in another part of the department. She may have been training a new sales associate. She may have been checking her department's financial performance against month-to-date projections. She may have been called on the carpet by *her* manager to explain her department's declining sales figures. Perhaps sales of watches in particular had fallen off.

So. . . Esther had other things to do? This is the excuse? This is the excuse that's offered in many cases today. As we said in our *Foreword*, managers today have to "wear many hats." They have many responsibilities. They can't be expected to be in several places at the same time. We simply can't afford, however, to offer this as an excuse. Somehow, there must have been a disconnect between Esther's "transmission" of what she expected of Sarah, and what Sarah interpreted to be her moment-to-moment responsibility behind the counter. Esther needs to own the responsibility for that disconnect, fix it, and guarantee (perhaps with the potential separation of Sarah from the company) that it never happens again.

In short, before Esther picked up another task in the store (see potential examples of what these might have been above), she should have ensured—"locked down"—in her list of priorities, with Sarah, what Sarah was supposed to do. The ensured act might have been: "Sarah will use her time productively, waiting on customers within seconds of when they arrive at the counter." This wasn't locked down, and now Caremart is locked out of our business.

But we need to be fair about this "locking down" idea, the idea that a manager can absolutely guarantee the responsible actions of her subordinates. We recall Colonel Jessup in the film "A Few Good Men," a movie that illustrates the locking down idea. Given the training and dedication U.S. Marines have, Colonel Jessup maintained that his men *couldn't* have disobeyed an order, one that led to the death of one of their cohorts. However, the film shows that even Marines, as human beings, demonstrate that people can and do disobey orders.

Still, I want to be way more certain that Esther did the locking down with Sarah that the officers in the film did with their men. Call me suspicious, but I think one of two things happened. First, Sarah didn't receive the order at all (to make customers the first priority); or, second, she failed to take that order seriously—a fault I'll continue to assign to Esther.

To review, the reason managers exist is to help organizations reach their goals and achieve their purposes. In Esther's case, her jewelry department is supposed to sell lots of watches. Sarah's failure to sell watches is Esther's failure. Esther needs to do better—at least with this one dimension of her job. If we can get her to read it, this book will help Esther manage *each* dimension of her job more effectively.

Before we leave this point, we need to acknowledge that sometimes the organization needs to share blame for individual employee performance. If not its fault entirely, sometimes an organization can tie a given manager's hands. This can happen through inadequate time to train associates, wages and incentives that fail to motivate both managers and associates properly, poor facilities, bad locations, and other factors that can affect individual performance.

As we will point out later however, these factors can't be offered as definitive reasons for substandard performance. Sometimes, as we will see, managers need to "manage up," engaging in behaviors that can mitigate both system (e.g. workflow) and organizational shortcomings. In fact, this is the conclusion that one of the accused soldiers in "A Few Good Men" comes to at the end of the movie. When his companion says the two of them weren't to blame for their fellow soldier's death (this soldier's name was Willie), the first soldier disagrees, saying in reference to the soldier who died, "We're supposed to look out for those who can't look out for themselves. We were supposed to look out for Willie." They could have "managed up," in other words, and they didn't.

A Framework for Improvement

Here's my prediction for you as a manager—and again, a "manager" is anyone who is charged with accomplishing an organization's purposes through the efforts of others. Your organization is not likely to deliver additional resources for you. You're not going to get more space, more people, nicer equipment, a shorter workweek, fewer regulations to comply with, more congenial co-managers, and certainly not a larger operating budget. Very likely you're on your own; you have to play the specific hand that you've been dealt.

The good news is that the hand you're holding is playable. And I do understand that you may already be playing it wonderfully well. If not, one difficulty you may be having is that you can't see all the cards clearly. Maybe there's an ace stuck behind a trey somewhere. Here's an idea that occurred to me a while back that could also be helpful.

I came up with this vision, this image years ago, of what my working life as a manager looked like. My vision was this. I saw myself as someone looking at a large, rectangular field. Along one edge of the field lay a row of beans—maybe they were kidney beans. I saw my job as moving those beans, one at a time, across the field—pushing each with the eraser end of a pencil. Eventually, my task was to move all of them across the field. I could leave no bean behind.

That was something of an "Aha!" moment for me. What that vision enabled me to do was "see" both the size and nature of the job that confronted me. My first recommendation for you is that you try to do this too: try to "see" your particular bean field more clearly. If you can't see it, I don't see how you can manage all of its component parts successfully.

Second, you need to understand that there are a lot of beans out there, perhaps more than you realized. Tired as you may be, you need to recognize that there are beans along the edge of the field that you haven't noticed. These unnoticed beans are there, and they may by this time be taking root. By the time you do see them, pushing them is going to be a lot more difficult. In our movie about the Marines, Willie turned out not to be "pushable" at all.

Third, moving different beans will require different tactics. You will be more comfortable working with some beans than with others. You will *like* moving certain beans and detest moving others. Perhaps Esther, for example, is more comfortable working with cost projections than she is with associate training. But there's no use pretending that a given bean isn't there. Like it or not, Esther has to acknowledge Bean Sarah and deal effectively with her (so Sarah in turn can deal effectively with me and my daughter—should she ever get another chance).

Fourth, the pencil you've been using may be inadequate as your only tool for moving the beans across the field. In addition to new tactics that you can employ with it (the pencil), you may well need to develop some additional tools, processes, and methods—and you may need to enlist some additional people—as you work to move each bean across the field. Not to just beat you senseless with this point, but the lesson of the "substandard" Marine in "A Few Good Men" applies here as well. Those in charge of Willie apparently needed other methods to help him succeed, and they didn't find them in time.

Fifth, having been given the position of manager (or foreman, or lead, or CEO), you may think you're done, that you've arrived as a manager. As articulated by Stephen Covey in his book *The 7 Habits of Highly Effective People*,[1] you may think that your title, what you *are*, somehow in and of itself should inspire your subordinates to perform as they should. It's not that way. Your success as a manager is going to involve your taking proactive, continuous, positive, directed *action* to make things better. What you *do*, in other words, is way more important than what you perceive yourself to *be*.

Let me leave you at the end of this chapter with another idea, one related to my very first point about "seeing" the scope of work that confronts you.

We've all put jigsaw puzzles together. Imagine for a moment that that's the task that confronts you. However, assume for the moment that the pieces of our hypothetical puzzle are scattered all over your house. What do you do? You go from room to room until you find all the pieces, putting them all into a box as you go. Having gone all through the house, at least now you have all the pieces in one place. You dump them out of the box, on your kitchen table, and begin to look for similar colors, parts of images, and similar shapes—all the pieces with straight edges for example.

Here's what would really help you in your effort to put the pieces of the puzzle together. It would really help you *if you could see the picture on the original box*. You would say, "Aha! That's what it's supposed to look like!" Then the pieces would come together more readily.

I want you to think of your job as a manager in that way. If you're having difficulties now, they may stem from the fact that no one has shown you the picture on the box.

For Further Consideration

1. Do you agree with the idea that management behavior in some organizations is less purposeful than it might be? Other than the "many hats" response, what else might we hear from organizations as to why this is the case?
2. Do you think the comparison of human organizations to insect colonies (bee hives and ant hills) is in any way accurate? Why/why not?
3. In this chapter Esther, Sarah's manager, is held accountable for Sarah's performance. Is this fair and reasonable? Are you held accountable for the actions of your direct reports? Are you able to "lock down," as we described it, the things your people are accountable for? How do you do that?
4. In your organization, how often, if at all, do either internal or external customers have to wait for service? How do you assess the impact of this on overall morale, productivity, and, eventually, profitability?
5. What are the beans that you have to push across the field every day? Which are ahead of others, and why?

6. Do you agree with the idea that what you do in your position is more important than the title or position you occupy? Why/why not? Give an example of your doing something vs. being something, and what the day-to-day impact your action in this area has.

7. In your position today, do you see the picture on the box clearly and completely? If not, what keeps you from doing so?

Notes

1. Covey, Stephen. *The 7 Habits of Highly Effective People*. New York: Free Press, 2004. Print.

2 HOW ARE WE DOING?

<u>Current State</u>

In our first chapter we considered the situation of Esther, our Jewelry Department Manager at Caremart. Let me say again that I know we may be judging Esther unfairly. She could be the most effective manager on the planet, and we experienced only a few moments of life in her department. Maybe that was the only time that a glitch like the one we had with Sarah ever occurred.

Unfortunately, it doesn't matter. It happened. And it's Esther's key responsibility as a manager to ensure that things like that *don't* happen. As we said, it violates the store's entire reason for being; it keeps Caremart from achieving its purpose. In a literal way, Esther didn't manage on purpose.

In Chapter One I went to some lengths to establish the idea that all of us managers have a lot to do—a lot of beans to push across the field. Lots on our plates. That notwithstanding, I need to ask you this necessary, but rather provocative question. It pertains to this chapter's purpose, which is to provide an overview of where we are with management. We're going to look at our current state, our condition. Part of this will include a look at our environment, our "milieu" (an early reviewer of this manuscript rebuked me for using a fancy word like "milieu"; I'm sorry, but the word fits!). This look at where we are in management will be augmented by looking as well at where we've been.

My provocative question is this: even with our full plates staring back at us, are we managers relevant? Are we necessary? Bear with me for a moment. I ask this question, for one thing, because more and more functions in the workplace are being automated. If you haven't visited a modern warehouse, you would be surprised to see many of the functions there that used to be carried out by people now carried out by machines. In a similar way, robots now do a great deal of the work on automobiles that used to be done by human beings. If you need an operation (say your gallbladder goes bad on you) that operation could be performed by a robot. We're relying more and more on computers and machines to do the work that people used to do, and managing people has always been the priority, the focus, and—to be honest here—the chief difficulty of those of us who choose management as a career.

I have other examples (we could discuss the publishing industry for example), but perhaps this is sufficient. Many tasks that used to be carried out by people are simply now carried out in other ways. Although I'm still afraid to use them, we even have those Self-Checkout stations in many large stores now. I don't trust them, but they are available.

Here is how I feel about this. While technology is continually remaking the working world, that world is still comprised of organizations. Those organizations are made up of people, systems, and processes grouped by function and task, and these organizations exist to carry out specific purposes. We still need human beings to make sense of all of the foregoing, and to make sure that people, systems and processes are aligned and working together in a meaningful way for the achievement of organizations' goals. In short, we still need managers; I think managers are still relevant. Granted, this "milieu" is very different than it was even ten years ago, but the central function of management is still intact, and the need for effective managers is still real.

Success Ratio

So we still need Esther there at Caremart. And while she may have had a minor slip up in the way she prepared Sarah to deal with me and my daughter, we're not going to give up on her. We need her; Caremart needs her. Her brief slip, however, does bring up another question.

This additional question is, while we've had the one example of Sarah and Esther, how are managers in general doing these days? Don't take this the wrong way (and get all sensitive on me), but I don't think we're doing as well as we might. Before you fly off the handle, let me ask you this (it's actually a two-part question): how are you doing as a manager? And, how many truly effective managers have you had in your working life?

Since I'm in charge of this book, I don't have to answer the first question—but how are *you* doing? I mentioned in the last chapter that you're not likely to get more pay, better equipment, more congenial co-managers, a larger budget— but aside from that, do you feel like you have the essential requirements of your position down pretty well? To some degree, current conditions are going to affect your answer, but in general, are things going well? My sense is that for all of us, again given the complexity of both the times we live in and the responsibilities we have, we're feeling a bit overwhelmed.

Now, about the second question—the effective managers we've had. What about that? Could you make a list for me, of those truly effective managers you've worked with? If I were to complete this exercise, I would end up with a very short list, and yours may be similarly short. I might come up with three or four names. When I say "manager," understand that I mean anyone who has the responsibility for accomplishing work through the efforts of other people. Thus my foremen and lead people in the corrugated plant I worked in a hundred years ago were managers, as was the plant superintendent.

How many names did you write down? What was it in their performance that led you to include them? The answers to that question are going to vary, I realize. I suspect that you'd say that some genuinely cared about you as a person; some had extraordinary technical skill and knowledge; some were expert at scheduling and organizing work; some were scrupulously fair and ethical; some would never ask you to do something that they weren't willing to do themselves.

Here's why I think these questions I've posed are relevant. If our goal through reading this book and other efforts is to improve as managers, wouldn't we seek first to emulate the successful managers each of us has had? Isn't it simply a matter of isolating their success qualities, and adapting those to ourselves?

Let me give you a firm "maybe" on that one. It just isn't that easy. Some say that effective management is only partly about individual human qualities. Further, if each of us who manages tries to cultivate some personal qualities that we don't now have, we may set ourselves up for disappointment. What worked for them may not work at all for us. This point is developed in Linda Martin and David Mutchler's *Fail-Safe Leadership*,[1] in which they elaborate the point that effective management is not about personal qualities (personal traits or attributes such as high morals or a brilliant mind), but about achieving results. I would say, to a degree. We can't say that ends justify means, but Martin and Mutchler make the valuable point that we can re-frame this question. We can emphasize results versus personal qualities that may or may not bring about the results we're looking for.

This is a complex point. I agree with Martin and Mutchler when they say we can't make management effectiveness totally about personality. In *The 7 Habits of Highly Effective People*, Stephen Covey talks a lot about this. He points up the difference between a so-called "personality ethic," based primarily on looks, glitz and quick fixes, versus his "character ethic," one based on time-tested principles. He says we need more of the latter and hardly any of the former if we want to be truly, lastingly effective as people and as managers. So for Covey, success *is* about a personal quality, that of strong, consistent, principled character.

The research that Jim Collins and his team did for *Good to Great*[2] does reveal a portrait of what they call Level 5 leadership, so they would concur I think that we *can* look for certain qualities to emulate. Here is what Collins says about these Level 5 leaders: "Level 5 leaders channel their ego needs away from themselves and into the larger goal of being a great company. It's not that Level 5 leaders have no ego or self-interest. Indeed, they are incredibly ambitious—*but their ambition is first and foremost for the institution, not themselves.*" (p. 21)   From this, we could say that "emulatable" qualities likely include both ambition and humility.

I used to look at the personality versus character equation when I interviewed teachers (yes, I used to be a teacher and a department chairman). In this role I interviewed and hired teachers, and also supervised student teachers. Teachers of course are managers; they manage a different "workforce" four or five times a day, depending on how many classes they teach. When I interviewed teachers, I learned not to be too impressed by what could be called surface qualities: looks, smile, the firm handshake, the laughing at all my jokes. This is because   what   students   respond   to   is   consistency, "sticktoitivity," and ultimately character. They want to know if you're going to be there tomorrow; that you'll do what you say you're going to do; if you're going to treat them fairly; that your evaluation of them will be clear and transparent— that there'll be no surprises at grading time.

In the early going here I simply want you to think about this question: who are the really good managers? What we'll want to do over the course of this book is have you keep your own manager/leader "profile" at the forefront of your consciousness. We're not looking for a Jekyll/Hyde trans- formation here; few of you really need to remake yourselves in order to be more successful in your manager role. Chapter 7, which is about managing change, is helpful in this area— helpful in terms of pointing out that we *can* change our profiles, in the process becoming more and more successful in the achievement of personal and organization goals. Again, by "profile" I mean the aggregate of personal qualities, tendencies, quirks, knowledge and skills that you bring to the table every day.

Qualifications and Characteristics

Let me state this again in regard to the relevance of and need for managers. We need them. Whenever a group of people comes together to achieve a given set of goals, someone needs to be there to organize and manage their efforts. Phillip Hunsaker in *Training in Management Skills*[3] says that all management activities divide themselves into four areas:

- Planning
- Organizing
- Leading
- Controlling

In other words, if a group coming together to achieve a set of goals lacks a plan, is disorganized, has no leadership and no strategy to keep it on track, it is not likely to achieve those goals. This is what effective management can provide.

Does anyone have much of a handle on this?—are many people skilled in the four areas that Hunsaker identifies? It looks to me as though coaches sometimes have this pretty well in hand. Consider, for example, a professional football team. An ownership team can establish a vision for the kind of team it wants to put on the field, and the team over time will come to represent or embody that vision. The ownership team hires a head coach who it thinks can do the operational things needed to bring the vision to life on the field.

This coach doesn't try to do everything on his own. He hires assistant coaches who oversee the work of different team functions. Offense and defense are divided into their component elements, and each of these elements comes to be presided over by a dedicated coach. On offense, an offensive coordinator oversees coaches for quarterbacks, running backs, receivers and offensive linemen, and similar divisions are set up on defense, "the other side of the ball."

Each coach has a purpose to achieve, all within the core vision of what the team aspires to be and what the team hopes to accomplish.

It all seems so simple, right? Perhaps the example of managing a football team is *too* simple? You as a manager might say, "Well yes, that's all well and good, but my operation has complexities that would drive football coaches crazy!" And in fact you may be right. In the rest of this chapter, we'll look at some reasons why you may in fact be right, some factors that are making all of our jobs as managers more difficult than they've ever been.

Let's first revisit the point about personal qualities and their impact on ineffective management. Let me repeat Martin and Mutchler's point, that you can't point to personality factors as the main ingredients in the effective management equation. They point out rightly that if it were a matter of personality, then all great managers and leaders would have the same profiles. They don't. Grant and Lee come to mind as great Civil War generals with wildly differing personalities. American presidents offer similarly different personality profiles. Consider business leaders as well, from flamboyant types such as Lee Iacocca and Donald Trump, to more reserved individuals identified by Jim Collins such as Darwin Smith of Kimberly-Clark and Colman Mockler of Gillette.

So we'll leave the "qualities" issue alone for a time. We'll acknowledge that individual human quirks, foibles, strengths and even pathologies play a role in manager success. In every age these basic human components that affect management performance are affected by prevailing social and economic conditions—in both good and bad ways.

Management in the Past

Prevailing social and economic conditions do not constitute *excuses* for ineffective management behavior, but they can provide partial explanations. The present moment in our working lives offers us a lengthy list of potential excuses and explanations.

When did it begin? Perhaps with the onset of vigorous foreign competition in what had been largely a competition-free environment. To choose an obvious example, consider the automobile industry. After World War II you could buy cars from only a handful of suppliers: GM, Ford, and Chrysler were the big three, and they had mild competition from companies such as Hudson and Studebaker (not that I'm old enough to remember this *personally*, you understand). We had few options from which to choose. Carmakers knew this, and offered us what they wanted to offer, in what colors, with what features, and at what price. We said basically, "Okay!"

The marketplace tended to be stable. People went to work for one company and stayed there, getting the gold watch and pension after putting in their thirty years. They were *valued* for putting in those thirty years. There was often loyalty on both sides of the employer/employee equation. While not enlightened, management was at least often benign.

All that changed. The era of increased, soon-to-be global competition brought with it increasing scrutiny of how things were done, and pressure increased to accomplish the most in the least amount of time and with the fewest number of people. We called all this re-engineering, "right-sizing," downsizing. The quality movement and lean manufacturing stressed just in time production and delivery (versus filling up warehouses with product and waiting for someone to order it) and an intense scrutiny of every facet of operation, with a squeezing out of every ounce of perceived fat that could be found.

And technology. Computers? Post War America did have computers, but they tended to consume entire rooms. Telephones? If you wanted to call someone, you called them on a land line. Some people may remember picking up dial-less telephones, and saying to an operator, "Give me 7694 please." The operator would connect that circuit, and you'd complete your call. I of course was not alive when this was happening. My sources, however, tell me that this is how it was. We lived in an internet-free, smart phone-free universe, one in which tweeting was still the sole province of birds.

No more. We dedicate a later chapter to technology that explores further how technology has come to affect us. Suffice to say at this point that technology now produces volumes of work and provides communication and other services that were previously unimaginable—all of which have complicated life tremendously for modern-day managers.

Let me conclude this section with a brief mention about the law. It too was different in what we could characterize as the good old days. The last century saw the establishment, rise, flourishing and later decline of the union movement. Not that unions aren't still with us. But when unions were at the height of their influence they simply played a much larger role in the way companies were managed than they do now. Their decline has been accompanied by an enormous increase in laws and regulations that provide protections for the workforce—protections once provided in part by union contracts. As a manager, you need to know much more about laws and regulations than formerly, and we address that need in part in Chapters Eleven through Thirteen.

Management and Diversity

We are not the country we were demographically. If we were once a melting pot, we are now more like a stew (we're in the same pot, but the ingredients in the pot are more clearly separable). Multi-culturalism is a fact of life; diversity in the country and in the workplace is a fact of life.

In addition to culturally and ethnically, we are also generationally diverse. People are working longer and longer, and the so-called "Veteran" generation born between 1920 and 1940 can find itself working with Boomers (1940-1960), Gen Xers (1960-1980) and now Millennials (1980-2000). In short, modern managers find themselves working with people who are perhaps 20 to 30 years older than they are, whose first language is not English, who are of a different color, and whose values vary widely from their own.

Families too are more diverse than they used to be (and yes, this does affect our lives as managers). I mentioned earlier that Post War America was a more stable time. It was in the sense that economic life was more stable, and that our national values were also more stable. Parents in my lower middle class neighborhood parented everyone's children. All of my neighborhood friends came from two-parent families. Many families went to church. When we grew to young adulthood we went to work, and pretty much "toed the line" once we got there. We knew that when our foremen and supervisors told us to do something, we were supposed to do it, and we usually did. We counted ourselves fortunate to have jobs.

Think about any handful of people who work for you. I don't want you to do this for EEO reasons (you can't go snooping into your people's family situations and ethnic identities—see Chapter Eleven), but consider how their personalities, values and ethics have been shaped by their families, by the communities in which they were raised. As we said above, some of these communities may have been in other countries. Some of these communities included (and include) gangs, and your employees may in fact still have gang affiliations. This was problematic in my work with a waste hauling firm. In one urban area we could only send certain gang-affiliated helpers on the backs of garbage trucks into neighborhoods friendly to them. Some, perhaps many of your employees come from single parent families. Some may have religious affiliations, some not.

We are not in Kansas anymore. Things are so different in so many different ways in the workplace that it's hard for us to count them. Perhaps other eras in our national history can match the diversity and complexity we now find in the workplace, but I find that hard to believe.

All of these societal and cultural factors color the picture you see on the box. They don't materially change that picture. What they do is point up all the more the need for a systematic approach (vs. a spontaneous one) to your work as a manager.

I summarize our status as managers this way. Far from being irrelevant, we are relevant as never before. In our current environment, characterized by diversity, change and uncertainty, the need is greater than ever for those who can see the picture whole, those who can make organized, systematic responses to that picture.

For Further Consideration

1. Whom would you describe as the most effective manager you've ever worked for? Why? Do you try to replicate this manager's approach in your own position today? Why/why not?
2. Is management relevant? Explain your answer.
3. While this chapter discusses many changes that have affected the workplaces, can you think of some that we've missed? What are they, and how have they affected the workplace in general, and yours in particular?
4. Some say that an individual manager's personal "make up" is less important than the results he or she achieves. Can any personality type or approach be successful, as

long as the affected work group is achieving its goals? Provide examples to support your answer.

5. In this chapter, the leadership hierarchy of a football team is outlined—with the overall approach coming from ownership, through the head coach, down through the efforts of all the assistant coaches. Is this model similar to the one you see operating in your organization? That is, how completely do the "assistant coaches" grasp and execute the approach of ownership and upper management?

6. This chapter reviews the major changes that have occurred in the life of American business over the past several decades. Have you seen major change affect your organization? If so, which do you think are most significant? Why? If not, how has your organization "escaped" the changes?

7. Is your organization diverse? How would you describe its employee demographic? What challenges and opportunities are available due to the diversity of your workforce? Give an example of both an opportunity and a challenge that you've dealt with: are you pleased with the results? Why/Why not?

Notes

1. Martin, Linda L., and Mutchler, David G. *Fail-Safe Leadership*. Orlando: Delta Books, 2003. Print.
2. Collins, Jim. *Good to Great*. New York: Collins, 2001. Print.
3. Hunsaker, Phillip L. *Training in Management Skills*. Upper Saddle River, New Jersey: Prentice-Hall, 2001. Print.

3 ASSESSING MANAGEMENT'S VALUE

Managing With a Full Plate

The factors and conditions described in the last chapter constitute multiple whammies in the lives of modern managers. Managers appear to have fewer and fewer resources and more and more responsibility to manage a workforce that is more and more diverse—with widely varying values and work ethics—while trying to stay current with more and more developments in technology. Any way you look at it, it's a full plate.

To return to our core topic, we could say in light of all of the above, that of course we have less successful managers today, managers who may not be delivering significant value to their organizations. How could we not? How can anyone manage at a high level in the face of the issues and difficulties outlined?

Sometimes the answer lies in organization. The football team analogy we used in the last chapter suggests that this may be true. Sometimes the organization of an enterprise is so tight that managers (or coaches in the football example) succeed seemingly by default. By "tight" I mean first of all that there may be proportionately more managers. If you have ten coaches for a population of sixty players (which could be the case with a pro football team), vs. say, three coaches for that same population, the numbers are definitely on your side. By the same token, each of those ten coaches/managers can be assigned to achieve proportionately fewer goals—with an increased likelihood of success.

The military is also instructive in this way. You have leadership and management at the squad, platoon, company, battalion and division levels. The chain of command is so rigid, and responsibilities so clearly understood within that chain, that failure at any level becomes rare. Value, in other words, would seem to be built in at the organizational level.

Geary Rummler and Alan Brache in IMPROVING PERFORM-ANCE: *Managing the White Space on the Organization Chart*[1] suggest that this is true, and they also point out the value of systems and well-defined processes in getting work organized and accomplished. If an organization is your standard "well-oiled machine," with all system parts clicking along, individual managers within that system have greater likelihood of succeeding. Difficulties in management often surface at the human level, and if systems and processes can minimize the potential for human error, the better the organization as a whole will function.

Sometimes success is possible through what could be called individual heroism. Even in the face of dwindling resources and complex, difficult responsibilities, individual managers "suck it up" and perform at high levels. Heroism however, is not the model that will sustain individual managers and the organization as a whole over time. Rummler and Brache point out that bad organizations and systems will defeat "heroic" individual performers every time.

Management as Value Proposition

For the moment we'll assume that a given manager is in fact working in a semblance of a well-oiled machine—and still not achieving optimum results. For the moment we'll lay aside organization and system issues, and put responsibility for performance squarely on the manager.

You would think—again given the complexity of the job as I've described it—that now more than ever managers would approach their day-to-day tasks with an agenda. By agenda I mean "orders"—descriptions of expected outcomes that reflect the vision and mission of the organization. You would think, logically, that upper management would have supplied managers with that agenda. You would think that individual managers would approach their days with purpose and intention, but this is not always the case.

Managers may not understand completely the concept of "value proposition" in terms of their relationships to their organizations. A value proposition suggests that value is being delivered in a particular way, value that exceeds that available through other means. For example, the value proposition in a maintenance department can be that existing equipment should be kept running at an agreed upon level for as long as possible, consuming as few human and material resources as possible. By "agreed upon level" I mean running at a set speed with an average number of shutdowns, each for an acceptable interval of time. We could argue over the wisdom of this approach as a value proposition, but you see my point: at least the organization is saying what it hopes to accomplish, at what price (in production speed, potential product quality and employee morale), and perhaps for how long (until this value proposition might prove untenable, and another would have to be implemented).

A value proposition that I see operating in many organizations today could be called "catching." Organizations appear to be saying, "For what we'll pay, we'll have managers 'catch' whatever surfaces in their departments." Maybe Esther back in Chapter 1 was a catcher, and this is why she didn't have time to monitor Sarah more closely. We can see why an organization might allow this kind of approach as a value proposition: an assistant manager to help Esther would cost more money, and there might not be room for that within Caremart's existing value proposition.

You can see the dangers in this approach. For one thing, it leads to life in the moment; it is, necessarily, reactive as opposed to proactive behavior. Maybe it's because of the complexity I outlined earlier; maybe there's just so much that can happen, so much possible difficulty ready to confront managers each day, that upper management perceives an agenda as having little value. In such an approach, whatever managers on the floor may plan to do would blow up in their faces anyway—so why bother? They'll *catch* things as those things come.

Of course there is every reason in the world to bother, to anticipate what may come and prepare systematically for it. Everything within the manager's purview must get done (all the beans must eventually be moved), but in fact rarely does everything get done. In addition to the value propositions they're being asked to execute, managers can fail to execute the full scope of their responsibilities for two reasons.

The first is that they rarely see the full scope of things they're responsible for on a given day (partly because they're "catching," which makes it difficult to see the rest of the picture on the box). The second is that, even when they do see what needs to be done, their approach to accomplishing it may be disorganized and inefficient—necessarily so, we could say, given the game plan some of them have been handed. Or they simply may lack the knowledge, skill and ability they need to handle each of their responsibilities. Of course things will slip through the cracks. Beans will go unseen, and some of them will take root.

We need more effective value propositions. We need to base them on careful, thorough assessments of how work is directed and performed. We need to ensure that work is possible for both employees and their managers. One way we do this is by showing each manager what we would like him or her to do, then ensure that he or she has the wherewithal to do it. Each manager will invariably have to do some catching, but catching should be the exception, not the norm. The norm should be planned, directed, intentional activity, activity supported by the time, dollars, tools, and personnel needed to execute it successfully. This is a value proposition that makes sense, one that is sustainable over time.

Accounting for Managers

I've said that effective management delivers value by seeing that an organization achieves its goals. Ineffective management injects negative value by keeping an organization from reaching those goals. Effective management is valuable because it greases skids, supporting and facilitating work, rather than hindering it. Ineffective management is value in reverse. It can throw wrenches into the gears; rather than being a remover of obstacles, it can itself be an obstacle.

It may be an obstacle, for example, in the way that it can affect profitability. In businesses and organizations, there are so-called individual contributors who actually produce work, and there are those who supervise work—those who ensure that the purposes of a work group, team, department, division, state or country get carried out. Sometimes these leaders are called "overseers"; they "see" that things get done.

What I want to explore in the paragraphs below is the concept of managers as assets or liabilities—literally as balance sheet items. They will be assets if they function effectively within sensible, logical value propositions; they will be liabilities if they don't. All of this is said with the caveat that the math in this particular equation is not completely of their own choosing. If someone is an effective manager asked to function in accordance with an unwieldy value proposition, the latter has the potential to reverse the equation—to turn that manager from an asset into a liability.

Managers are usually classified as "indirect" labor. "Direct" and "indirect" labor are accounting terms for employees. One group is directly involved in the delivery of goods and services (these are the "direct" people), and the other group is not (these are the "indirect" people). Indirect labor, when expressed in dollar terms, contributes to an organization's fixed or ongoing costs.

When you subtract direct labor and the other costs directly associated with producing goods and services (e.g. costs for raw materials), you get a figure called "gross profit." To arrive at the bottom line for a business—"net profit"—you subtract fixed costs (operating expenses), plus any interest expense the business incurs, plus taxes, depreciation and amortization. Depreciation accounts for the diminishing value of fixed assets over time, such as buildings and equipment, and amortization for the diminishing value of "intangible" assets such as patents over time.

A business's fixed costs are also referred to as overhead. Energy costs, rent and utilities are all included in overhead. These are all referred to as fixed costs because they are incurred no matter how much or how little revenue comes into the company from sales or investment. To maximize profits, companies try to keep fixed or overhead costs as low as possible.

Consider, for example, the fixed costs of a retail clothing store. Square footage and shelf space are important to such an operation. In order to justify increasing its operating space from, say 1,000 square feet to 1,500 square feet, store management would have to explain how that extra space would enable the store to realize a corresponding gain in revenue and profit. In a similar way, if ownership of the store decided that it could no longer operate with one manager but actually needed two, it would need to justify that additional overhead cost. Additional management in this case, as a component of overhead, would have to be justified in terms of its commensurate *value*. From our investment in management in general (not just in this example), we should realize at least proportionate value in return for the dollars we invest.

Managers and Machines

Objectively, we can compare the performance of managers to the employment of equipment. As suggested above, managers are organizational assets in the same way that machines and file cabinets are. If an organization invests heavily in equipment, it must recoup that investment through optimum use of it. For example, assume that a construction company buys a new bulldozer, hopefully one that augments the capability of its existing "fleet."

Once they've invested tens of thousands of dollars in the new bulldozer, they must put it to work! It must "earn its keep," so to speak, by accomplishing substantial work for the organization. We hope that the company has done its due diligence, completing a cost/benefit analysis before going forward with the purchase of the bulldozer (comparing the cost of the bulldozer over time against the anticipated increase in revenue it could provide).

In short, the bulldozer will justify itself over time through the increased tons of earth it will move, perhaps through substantial savings in maintenance, and perhaps through additional savings in man hours (one operator should be able to achieve greater productivity with the new machine than with an older, less reliable machine with less earth moving capacity). Upper management will say "Sure it was expensive, but here's the additional profit we'll realize from it over time."

Since dollars are so tight today, you would think that upper management would scrutinize every aspect of company performance—including management performance—more rigorously than ever. You would think they'd say "Sure, Martinez is costing us $120,000 annually in salary and benefits, but here is the specific value we're getting in return." Maybe they've calculated value that way, but the proof is rarely in the proverbial pudding.

Demonstrating Value

How do you as a manager do a cost/benefit analysis on yourself? How do you get clarity around the value proposition you're asked to occupy? The first thing I would do is come to understand the metrics management is using to calculate success: units sold, quality complaints received, employee turnover, labor hours to budget, miles of track laid, widgets assembled, safety records set—and so on and on.

Then I would clarify my contribution to each of those metrics. Employee turnover in the preceding six months was 6 percent. You initiated three employee relations initiatives in the last six months, and employee turnover dropped to 3 percent. The cost to replace each employee in your department is calculated to be $5,000, so you can say that you contributed to a savings of $15,000. You make similar calculations for other variables.

At the end of the day you should be able to say, "For the aggregate $40,000 I was paid from January through June, my department realized revenue enhancements and cost savings of $80,000, giving the organization a cost/benefit ratio of 100% for the dollars it invested in me." Then you would be in a position—if you chose to—to put another value proposition in front of your manager. You could say, "I think these numbers speak for themselves, but if we had two more operators, an additional lead person and the automatic conveyor I've recommended for Line 2, the increase you see would increase by another 25 percent."

When I do consulting work with companies, especially on matters involving organizational development, my dream is always for the chief stakeholder in the organization to be able to walk into the office of a manager—say a department manager—and ask that manager what he or she is doing.

My dream is for the subordinate manager to cite chapter and verse about what he or she is doing (as in the example above). I don't want to hear about multi-tasking. The fact that everyone has a lot to do is often a copout, an excuse to do either nothing or nothing of consequence. There should be one thing on that subordinate manager's desk and on her mind. She should say to her superior, "Expenses for uniforms last month were 20% higher than our projection, and I'm reviewing both our data and the provider's invoice to see if I can find where the discrepancy is coming from." This point will be elaborated further in Chapter Nine, "Managers and Finance."

In my experience we don't require the kind of accountability just discussed from our managers. We have a sense that they're doing something, but rarely can any of us say specifically what that something consists of—nor what value that activity is bringing to the organization. Worse, sometimes the highest ranking members of an organization's executive team cannot say with any specificity, moment to moment, what *they* are doing to move the organization forward. And that behavior is of no more value to the organization than that of a new bulldozer sitting idle in a parking lot.

This being able to explain (justify) what you're doing isn't a new concept. It is very like Management By Objectives (MBO), something we've known about and practiced to varying degrees for more than half-a-century (the idea came from

Peter Drucker in the 1950's)[2]. In fact we see the outline and at least the sporadic practice of MBO often in organizations, as goals are set and then "cascaded" through the organization. When used as designed, MBO can give all stakeholders in an organization the feeling that they're a part of things, that their execution of their piece of the overall plan matters.

Aubrey Daniels in *PERFORMANCE MANAGEMENT: Improving Quality Productivity through Positive Reinforcement,*[3] talks about the need to "pinpoint" exactly the behaviors we want and need from the workforce. Rummler and Brache describe the need to specify expected performance at three levels: organization, process, and individual performer. Michael Gerber in *The E-Myth Revisited* [4] emphasizes the need for managers to complete position agreements in which they describe the actual activities they're to be accountable for.

Some may say that while these are helpful theories, things have simply begun to move too fast for them to work as designed—change happens too rapidly. What seems like a worthy, doable goal at the start of a performance cycle all of a sudden becomes unimportant or even impossible. I don't buy this argument. The methods described above can have needed flexibility built into them. The subordinate we visited earlier can say to her boss, "I was working on the annex plans that we drew up in March, but the weather we had combined with the union work stoppage caused us to go another route; I'm working on an RFP now for bids to expand usable space in the B Building." Aubrey Daniels would say that the sub-ordinate substituted one appropriate "pinpoint" of expected behavior for another.

But my sense is that the chief stakeholder won't hear this or any other pinpoint. The subordinate manager instead will say "Oh, you know—same old same old!" This is supposed to mean something. The chief stakeholder will smile, nod, and say, "Well, hang in there!"

Now that *does* mean something. It means that there is no pinpoint, no agenda, no plan, and that nothing specific is in the works—and that all of the foregoing is okay. It is value proposition by chance. I don't understand the value of "same old, same old."

"Hanging in there" as status quo—as acceptable performance—rarely delivers measurable, consistent value, value that the organization urgently needs from its managers in order to survive and prosper.

For Further Consideration

1. Organizational structure is important to the amount and quality of work that gets done, as are operating systems within various departments and work groups. How do you assess your organization in this regard? If you could create a new design for the organization, what would it look like? What system changes (e.g. procedures) would you make, and why?
2. This chapter suggests that managers sometimes fail to see the full range of their responsibilities. Do you think this is accurate? Can you recall being reminded of a responsibility you didn't know you had? What kept you from being aware of it?

3. How do you assess overhead—fixed costs—in your organization? If you assess it as high, do you see ways to reduce it? What are some of them?

4. Put the concept of "value proposition" in your own words.

5. Refer back to the example of the manager suggesting an additional 25 percent in value that he could accrue for the organization. Have you ever tried to set up a similar calculation—one that would demonstrate in a concrete way the value you bring to the organization? If you were to do so now, what variables would you include in your calculation?

6. Is it reasonable to assess the value of a manager the same way you assess the value of a copier or computer application? Why/why not?

7. Is a version of Management by Objectives (MBO) operating in your organization? If so, and if you could "tweak" the way it's operating, how would you change it? Why?

8. Do you agree that the "Same old same old" mentality is at work in many organizations? If so, is it reasonable to expect that it can be changed? Why do you think some managers prefer "Same old same old" to other approaches?

Notes

1. Brache, Alan P., and Rummler, Geary A. *IMPROVING PERFORMANCE: How to Manage the White Space on the Organization Chart*. San Francisco: Jossey-Bass, 1990. Print.

2. Drucker, Peter. *The Practice of Management*. New York: Harper, 1954. Print.

3. Daniels, Aubrey C., Ph.D. *PERFORMANCE MANAGEMENT: Improving Quality Productivity Through Positive Reinforcement*. Tucker, Georgia: Performance Management Publications, 1989. Print.
4. Gerber, Michael E. The E-Myth Revisited. New York: HarperCollins, 1995. Print.

4 THE MYTH OF MULTI-TASKING

The Importance of Perception

A line in the hymn *Amazing Grace* is "I once was lost, but now am found—was blind, but now I see." The idea of course is that the speaker wasn't physically blind, but didn't understand or grasp the importance of life until he saw the errors in one way of living, and the rewards of another. He couldn't live one way until he "saw" another way to live.

Sometimes learning another way to see is a matter of simple perception. We can learn to look at a picture of something and see something completely different than we'd seen before. Stephen Covey uses the picture on the next page to illustrate this point.

This can be a picture of an old woman. She is looking ahead or slightly left as we view the picture. She has a prominent nose, and her mouth is little more than a slit, just above her pointed chin. We see her primarily in profile.

Or, it can be a picture of a young woman. She is turned almost completely to the right as we view the picture. Her left cheek and jaw are the old woman's nose. All we see of her left eye is an eyelash, and we can barely make out the tip of her nose.

When people suddenly see the "other" image, they usually shout out "Aha! Now I see!"

I hope that something like this awareness can happen as we discuss our vision of "management." In any management role, over time, we can become focused on too few of the duties and responsibilities that confront us every day. Sometimes this takes the form of worry over what one or more stakeholders thinks of us. We find ourselves, if not obsessing, at least concentrating more than we need to about these peoples' opinions—to the neglect of other things that require our attention. A book of some years ago by Terry Cole Whitaker that helped me in this regard was titled *What You Think of Me Is None of My Business*.[1]

Or, we can gravitate toward the duties, responsibilities and activities that we like the most and are the most familiar with. If we're mechanically inclined, we want to dive into problems with machinery and equipment, and help the maintenance people get things running properly (whether they want our help or not). If we're "numbers people," we want to stay in the office and pore over spreadsheets. If we're more social, we want to be out on the floor with our people, making sure that they're all okay (and that we're okay). If we're "techies," we need to have the newest version of each device and application. I sometimes see the latter as the tail wagging the dog. Which came first, the manager or the smart phone? Sometimes it appears that the human being is being swallowed by the technology.

These examples suggest that we can fall into predictable ruts in the performance of our management duties, and I recommend that we guard against this tendency.

Since we often gravitate toward those parts of our jobs that we find most comfortable, it is something of a myth to say that we "multi-task"—pay attention equally to a number of competing demands—when in fact we may pay only lip service to a number of those demands. We could say that we are partial-tasking rather than truly multi-tasking.

None of the specific dimensions of our jobs that we are drawn to are necessarily bad of course. I return, however, to *all* the beans, and to all the things we need to be and all the things we need to do to keep them inching along. We may have been "seeing" our role in just one or two key ways, and we need to see all the roles, all the duties and responsibilities.

To be more effective as managers—to deliver the value we talked about in the last chapter—we need to see the whole picture—the "picture on the box" that we described in

Chapter One. In gravitating toward the activities, responsibilities and perhaps the people you perceive as most important and/or enjoyable and meaningful, you may have been looking at a picture on the box that has a bunch of pieces missing. Whether they're down in the basement or somewhere else, you need to find them and put them in the puzzle—so that a complete and accurate picture emerges.

Let me give you what I hope won't be a laughably simple example. If you manage a group of sales people, you're responsible for managing all of them. You like Herb, so you spend a lot of time with him, perhaps even socializing with him away from work. Donna is something else again. You've just never been able to warm up to her. She doesn't move as many units as Herb, and just seems to be sulky all the time. Perhaps worse, she doesn't seem to "get" you. She doesn't laugh in the right places; she doesn't take your suggestions to heart as to how she can improve.

In this example, your attention paid to Herb, nice as it is for you, is a rut that you're in. The attention you're *not* paying to Donna is going to jump up one day and bite you in the backside. Get up, get over there, and find out how she's doing.

<u>Management Tools</u>

When we speak of management dimensions, we're talking about two things. First, there's the picture on the box itself: That's no longer a simple stick figure seen against a blank backdrop. I've seen pictures showing managers with multiple arms (like an octopus), each holding a different tool—a hammer, a measuring tape, a screwdriver, and so on--and while these are meant to be humorous, they do convey a point. Managers really do need a variety of tools to complete the jobs they confront every day.

In addition to practical hand tools such as saws and wire cutters, managers need at different times:

- A psychiatrist's couch
- An accountant's ledger (or an application like Quick-books)
- A computer
- A smart phone
- A copy of *How to Win Friends and Influence People*
- An organization chart
- The company's annual report
- The company's business plan
- Financial reports
- The company's safety program
- Product specifications
- A policy manual and employee handbook
- Training programs
- A current copy of the Federal Register
- Other (put in your job-specific components here)

We have a lot to do, and doing it effectively requires us to use tools like those above—and many others that I didn't name. The sheer multiplicity of these tools adds even more to the full plate we've been talking about.

To return to my focus in this chapter—multi-tasking— how do you feel about the possibility of doing more than one thing at a time? I call this chapter "The *Myth* of Multi-tasking," but wouldn't we be *truly* multi-tasking (doing two or more things simultaneously) if we could move more than one of our beans at a time a bit farther across the field? Let me answer this question by telling a brief story.

An Example of Multi-tasking

I once had the great misfortune to have my car break down on a desolate stretch of mountain road. I was picked up in the early hours of the morning by the driver of a large tractor trailer. To my chagrin, the driver, more or less simultaneously, was: talking to me; turning to look at me as he talked; watching the road; talking on a CB radio; watching the instrument panel; discussing politics; drinking beer; driving the truck (which had its own multiplicity of tasks—steering, shifting, braking); and petting a dog on the floor between us.

In a real sense his accomplishment of all these tasks wasn't "mythological" at all; he really did all of them, and he got me safely to my destination.

Part of me resists accepting this fact. I want to conclude that multi-tasking is a myth because we *can't* really do more than one thing at a time. Except, as my truck driving friend illustrated, we can. Granted, in a physical sense, it's difficult to do more than one thing at a time. The more dextrous we are, again as the driver demonstrated, the more physical tasks we are able to juggle and actually accomplish—to a point. We can't rake leaves and paint seascapes, for example, at the same moment in time. In any role or task that we undertake, however, there are at least two activities going on: one is the physical task in front of us, such as performing a brake job or balancing our checkbook, and two is the mental activity going on in our heads.

Remember Captain Sullenberger, the airline pilot who, in January of 2009, landed his jetliner in the Hudson River— saving the lives of all those on board. Think about his "repertory of responses" when he realized that his plane was malfunctioning. He needed to pay attention, almost simultaneously, to all the readings he was getting from his instruments. He needed to manipulate all the controls at his fingertips. And most importantly, he needed to *think* about what would be the single most appropriate course of action to take in that situation.

Both my truck driver and Captain Sullenberger were "response-able." Each selected from among a range of potential responses and then acted accordingly to carry out one overriding responsibility: the driver to keep the truck on the road, Captain Sullenberger to land the plane in the river. Each had to be aware of the range of responses available to him; each needed to exercise judgment as to which to act on and when; and finally each needed the physical dexterity to carry out what he deemed to be the moment-to-moment requirements of his respective situation.

My first conclusion is that to be successful in the respective roles of our lives (including our roles as managers), we need to have as broad a vision as possible of what *could* confront us in the performance of a given role. This is the complete picture on the box I keep talking about. Let me hammer this "complete" idea even more. Consider an air traffic controller. Does an air traffic controller get to choose which planes to address, either those landing or those taking off? I think not. In just this way, you don't get to pick and choose among the items on *your* plate. You have to see all of them; you have to interact with all of them.

Second, we need to be aware of the potential to act that we bring to any given situation. Each of us is potential waiting to be transformed into action. The more resource-full we can be, that is the more "full of resources" we can become, the more response-*able* we become. We will not only deal with *all* of those planes coming and going, we'll do so skillfully and economically.

This awareness or readiness to act is really the point—not so much the discrete actions that we can characterize as multi-tasking in any given instance.

I forget where I heard this phrase, but I like the idea of "dynamic equilibrium." What this means to me is that no "performer" can approach his/her specialty in a rigid, "one note" manner. We can't, to put it another way, box flat-footed; we need to be up there on the balls of our feet, ready to hook, jab, uppercut, feint or protect ourselves as the moment in the round requires. In this sense, once again it isn't the discrete tasks that we can perform moment-to-moment that are the real point: the real point is the state of *sustained readiness* we bring to the situation as a whole. This is what you need to develop as a manager. Like Hamlet, you need to realize and act on the principle that "the readiness is all."

What "multi-tasking" really refers to is the combination of thought and action. We can pull weeds, for example, while we think about the problems our children are having in history class. In this sense you as a manager need to pay attention carefully to your thought life on the job. You can indeed be taking care of one dimension of your job (in your mind thinking through how you're going to handle a discipline problem) while you help change the dye in a press. Do not, however, get your hand caught in the press as you think about the disciplinary problem!

In one sense it's a matter of learning how to pay attention, to focus on one task while retaining awareness of and even processing thoughts about others. Now in the case of the air traffic controller, he or she has learned to focus very *quickly* and successfully on one plane at a time. So "agile" are air traffic controllers that they can look like they're truly multi-tasking, but they're really doing one thing—one plane—at a time. They're just doing it at warp speed, something that they've learned how to do over time.

A second point to keep in mind is that you can't think about and act on everything yourself. You need to look around for assistance, perhaps from technology and from other people. Multiple things can be happening, in other words, while you're working on that dye in the press. An assistant can be updating files; an answering machine can be recording incoming calls; the safety manager can be creating the agenda for the next safety meeting. You do not have to be everywhere at once, and you don't have to be physically doing everything yourself. Delegation; there's part of your answer.

Remember too that given the complexity (i.e. the many-sidedness) and what we could call the "fluidity" of the workplace, none of us can afford to settle into one or more of the ruts I alluded to earlier. All of us have seen managers in these ruts or "channels." Not only do many settle into just a few of them (i.e. the numbers, the processes, the technology), but they also settle into just a few attitudes or "postures" as they go about their business.

By "posture" I mean what we could call a "persona," or a role. Managers can become not exactly caricatures, but they can come to resemble specific types: "My Way or the Highway"; "Mr. Sensitivity"; "Production Uber Alles"; "I Just Want People to Like Me"; and so on.

If you may have fallen into one of these roles or postures, you may need to back out of it. Each of us needs to be who we are. And we are, as I've been saying, housed in our unique personalities, bundles of potential. Bundles of "response-abilities," with all kinds of successful responses waiting to be summoned. We can't hinder this potential behind one rigid idea of what we like to do or who we want to be. Again, remember Hamlet and that readiness idea.

<u>Management "Content"</u>

I describe the modern workplace as "fluid." This means that it has the capacity and the need to change—that it *does* change rapidly, and as we just saw, managers need to be ready to adapt. One catchword that describes this management quality is "agility." We managers need to be "agile" (up there on the balls of our feet) in the face of the magnitude, variety and volatility that characterize the workplace. I think of frogs, leaping from lily pad to lily pad. In the space below, I'm going to describe what some of the "pads" are that we need to land on and occupy.

The following individual topics all receive treatment later in dedicated chapters. These are some of the major areas (dimensions) of your working life that you need to affect as a manager, that you need to retain a "dynamic readiness" to act on. These are "potentials" for which you need to become resource-full.

- **People**. Many say that managing people is the most complex and challenging aspect of their jobs, and they're right. In my life in a public school, we used to say how wonderful the job would be if it weren't for the kids, and we might say the same about the workplace and employees. People embody the greatest potential for success in your operation, and they comprise at the same time the greatest potential for varying degrees of failure. We need to learn how to relate to our employees, all of them. If you consider yourself a loner, develop another idea of yourself, because that one isn't going to be productive. You need to develop sociability; you need to become a communicator, a motivator, an influencer, an inspirer.

- **Money**. You manage money in the sense that you're to use the resources at your disposal (man hours, raw material, equipment, locations) in the most cost effective way possible. You're supposed to eliminate waste and manage lean. You're also supposed to understand your budget and manage to that budget. If you don't know them already, you'll have to learn the basic financial reports that indicate how well you're doing. It is so tempting for me to say here that you have to become a bean counter—making a connection to those beans lying along the edge of the field. But of course I'm above that.

- **Planning**. This dimension flows through all the others. This is what you do instead of "catch" as it was described in Chapter Three. The value proposition that you create and embody requires that you arrive at work every day with a plan in mind (and in your computer), one that enables you to address each dimension of your job successfully, one that will affect considerably the quality of sleep you get each night. While being extremely agile, you do recognize the need to map out those pads, formulating at least a rough idea of which you'll leap to, what you'll do once there, and how long you'll stay. Don't tell me that planning doesn't work for you, that your job is too fast-paced and hectic. You can learn to plan, and you will.

- **Compliance**. I hope you have some idea of how highly regulated the workplace is. The EEO laws are only a part of it, albeit perhaps the most important part. Safety is hugely important; as an agent of the company you're responsible for ensuring a safe and healthy workplace for your people. You need to ensure that your employees have a legal right to work in this country. You need to ensure that no one steals their identity. You need to guard their medical information. Ignore this part of your responsibility only if you want to pay substantial fines and perhaps go to jail.

- **Technology.** Part of me wants to bring technology to a screaming halt, to return to a simpler time. This is not going to happen. Technology is here and it isn't leaving— in fact, its cousins are arriving *en masse* tomorrow. There is no room for dinosaurs in the workplace anymore. Even though technology changes minute-by-minute, you owe it to yourself and to your organization to stay on top of it as best you can, to put it to work as best you can in your specific area of responsibility. You need to occupy a middle ground between full-fledged geek- or nerd-dom and out-of-date dinosaurosity. Yes, there is such a word as "dinosaurosity."

- **Risk.** Risk can be a component of compliance, but it also has a life of its own. Managers are responsible for acting effectively in the face of any number of emergencies: what do you do in the event of a fire? An explosion? A chemical release? What if an individual enters the workplace with a gun? What if your employees reveal incriminating information, either about themselves or something that's happening in their working lives? As much as we'd like to sweep these kinds of things under the rug, we risk our own futures and those of our organizations if we do.

- **Service**. In this chapter I make the point that a service mentality is that—a mentality or frame of reference— more than it is a "dimension." I do have a bias in this area. To me the service orientation needs to infuse everything we do in the workplace. I don't think any of you readers are out there alone in your respective workplaces. There are people upstream and downstream of you in your organizations; there are customers and suppliers, regulators and the community at large. Your role is to deliver services to all of them—and not begrudgingly! As we'll see, humility and a service mentality are central to personal and organizational success.

- **Discipline and Accountability**. As managers we *are* disciplined and we do our best to develop that quality in the people around us. Further, we need to dispense or administer discipline (positive and negative consequences for performance) to those who work with and for us. We are also accountable (responsible) for all of our actions in the workplace. Bucks stop with us. I make the point in this chapter that neither of these qualities, discipline and accountability, is possible without the other. I'll keep you in suspense as to how that works until you read Chapter Sixteen.

- **Leadership**. People often find it instructive to separate the qualities and responsibilities of leaders from those of managers. Leaders are said to establish vision and purpose, and managers to engage in the day-to-day tasks of bringing vision and purpose into reality. While there's some value in making the distinction between leaders and managers, in fact both leadership and managerial ability are needed to bring out the best in people. You, in other words are going to be a leader/manager. This dual nature—this requirement—applies regardless of the titles people have, and whether their offices are in the C Suite or adjacent to the shop floor.

A scary thought is that this isn't a complete list. It may be complete enough, however, to make my point: you can't "see" just one aspect of your job at the expense of all the others. The dimensions of management multiply for entrepreneurs—owners/managers of their own businesses. You people may think of yourselves as Lone Rangers as you face your unique challenges. You may think that no one understands the business that you're in the way you understand it, and in a way you're right. What you really mean, most of the time, is that no one understands the *content* of your business the way you do. You understand the content side of electronics, or used cars, or landscaping, or baking.

But if you're successful in today's business climate, you may be succeeding in spite of yourself, not because of yourself. Again, you were drawn to the content of your particular business, and naturally you want to focus on that—and get into the ruts or channels we talked about earlier. Not to sound like the proverbial broken record, but look again at the dimensions I listed above: you as an entrepreneur especially need to take a long look at *all* of those; begin focusing now on those that may need additional attention. And if you do find yourself in a channel, you need to at least stop digging!

Indicators and Controls

Have you ever seen the cockpit of an airliner? What Captain Sullenberger looked at as he prepared to land the plane in the river? Most of us would be discombobulated indeed at the array of gauges, dials, instruments, levers and switches found there. Before taking off, pilots and copilots work through a preflight checklist, making sure that the readings they see on their airplanes' "dashboards" are in the required ranges. The cockpit also includes the alarms needed to alert pilots if anything goes wrong with the airplane during flight.

These instruments, alarms and controls function at least in part like the picture on the box I've been describing: they indicate what you need to pay attention to, what you need to develop the readiness to act on. Of course the pilot looks out the windshield to see other elements of the picture as the flight progresses.

What I'm trying to provide you in this book is something like this cockpit: a place where you can identify all the things that may affect you in flight each day as a manager—as you "pilot" your business or organization. I like the analogy, because, just like the pilot, if you don't "see" all the gauges and potential alarms, bad things can happen. I remember praying fervently that my truck driver would pay attention to the right things in his cockpit—the things that would keep us safely on the road.

It would be convenient if each of us could step into a cockpit like that of an airliner and be handed our pre-flight checklist. That isn't the case. Our respective cockpits are the workplaces we occupy, and we need to configure those as best we can to give us the readings and alarms we need. Perhaps our pre-flight checklist will be a pencil and paper to-do list. Maybe it's an electronic to-do list on your computer or iPad. Maybe it's a list you hand your administrative assistant, along with instructions as to how he or she is to remind you of all that's on your plate. Maybe you have file folders for each dimension of your job in racks on your desk, color-coded by each function you're required to perform.

One indicator in your cockpit is the thought life that I alluded to earlier. Have you seen the ticker used at the New York Stock Exchange—the way changing stock prices flow by in a continuous stream? To me that isn't unlike our thought life. We need to exercise control over that. We need to show and react only to those stocks reflected in the Dow Industrials, so to speak—not the universe of stock performance that we could pay attention to and react to. We'll describe a way to filter and screen these "inputs" we think about in the next chapter.

Your cockpit is where you see the picture on the box. It's where each dimension of your job must be visible to you. Each must have a control mechanism or mechanisms that you can use during the course of the day. You need to "see" all of the dimensions of your job, ALL the things that could cause the plane to lose power, and you need to have the instruments at your fingertips to control them. If each of us can get our respective cockpits designed and outfitted correctly, we should be more comfortable and assured pilots than we are now.

For Further Consideration

1. Do you recall having an "Aha!" moment?—an occasion in which you suddenly came to see something in a radically different light? Describe that situation, and what its impact on you has been.

2. Do you "get" the "dynamic equilibrium" concept? How would you describe the "readiness to act" that you bring to the workplace every day?

3. Have you experienced "My Way or the Highway" management? How did you respond to it? In your life as a manager, have you used this approach? When, if ever, might it be not only appropriate, but necessary?

4. What is your "agility quotient"? That is, how easily are you able to balance competing demands, putting down one task and very quickly picking up another? Are there any times when "agility" turns into the dreaded chicken with its head cut off syndrome? How do you keep this from happening?

5. Does the "cockpit" analogy work for you? Why/why not? In your management role, do you have a "dashboard" that helps you identify issues requiring your attention? If so, how would you describe it? If you could make changes to it, what would they be?

6. This chapter lists some of the prominent dimensions of a manager's job—People, Money, Compliance, and so on.

Are some of these more challenging for you than others? Why?

7. In a similar way, which dimensions of your job are most satisfying to you? Why do you think this is the case? As you engage in them, can any qualify as ruts or channels as we described them? If so, what have been some effects or consequences of your occupying them?

8. Thinking about your various areas of responsibility, do you have help in carrying any of them out? Where does this help come from? Do any issues arise in the process? If so, how do you typically resolve the issues?

9. Are there dimensions of your job that are not listed in this chapter? What are they? What challenges, if any, do you encounter in dealing with them?

<u>Notes</u>

1. Cole-Whitaker, Terry. *What You Think of Me is None of My Business*. New York: Penguin Group, 1988. Print.

5 FILTERS AND SCREENS

<u>Common Denominators</u>

Those of you reading this book may be one of the following:

- You're a department manager in a production facility. You could be a quality manager, a safety manager, a maintenance manager, an environmental manager or a production manager.
- You're a manager in a retail operation (think Caremart).
- You're a first-line supervisor in any kind of business, industry, or nonprofit organization.
- You're a pastor or associate pastor.
- You're a foreman or lead in a manufacturing or process industry.
- You're the owner, chief cook and bottle washer of your own company.
- You're a school administrator: a controller, a transportation coordinator, a superintendent, a principal, a department chairperson.

- You work in local, state, or national government, managing one or more functional areas such as purchasing, transportation, or distribution.
- You're a resident of a company's C-Suite: a CEO, COO, CFO, CIO.

All of the individuals named above face the challenges and opportunities we're talking about in this book. All of them face the dimensions of the management job that I outlined in the last chapter.

What unites all of us as managers is the complexity that faces each of us. If something is complex, that means it has a lot of different parts or pieces to it. Each of our jobs is complex, of course, in its own way. Supervisors on a manufacturing floor have a different "plateful" to deal with each day than does, for example, a Lutheran associate pastor.

A number of things unite us, however—what we can call the common denominators that exist no matter what kind of managers we are. The most important of these is purpose, and I've said this several times in the foregoing chapters: we are all charged with the responsibility of moving our respective organizations forward.

We outlined some of the common denominators in the last chapter: whether we are church volunteers or shop supervisors, we need to accomplish goals through the efforts of other people. We need to recognize laws that affect our respective workplaces, and make sure that we are in compliance with them. It has gone unsaid so far, but we need specialized knowledge of the organizations we find ourselves in. This last point has been debated some, with one side saying that, once schooled in effective management, a manager can step into a management role in any organization.

Having seen that idea put into action, I'm not so sure. Of course organization content can be learned (i.e., library science, electronics, packaging, warehousing), and there's even something to be said for bringing in a manager "cold"— one who hasn't had the time or the opportunity to develop bad habits. I think, on balance, that organization knowledge is a good thing. The more we speak the language of our constituents, the more we can match up our abilities with theirs, the more readily they can accept and take direction from us.

The other common denominators have to do with areas such as planning, scheduling, human resources, some form of financial management, and so on. Again, we listed these basic factors in the last chapter to give you what amounts to advanced warning of what comes next in the book. To say this another way, the picture on the box for each of is going to be different, in that some will have spruce trees versus palm trees, but each will have trees. We are to develop the "dynamic equilibrium" we need, along with the "response-ability" required, to deal effectively with whatever flora and fauna we see around us.

Processing Inputs

Common to all of our varied experiences as managers is this. A lot of things come at us during the course of the day. This idea is so important that I'm going to repeat it, and I'm going to give it a paragraph all its own.

A lot of things come at us during the course of the day.

I remind you of this idea throughout the book. I try to give you comparisons—metaphors—that help you visualize your role and the things that "come at you." I'm going to call these things that come at us "inputs." My question for you is, does it actually feel like a number of things are coming at you? Or is your workplace a fairly placid, predictable place? By contrast, I perceive that things do "blow at us," as in a windstorm. I picture scenes of hurricanes and tornadoes. I realize that this is a rough, overly dramatic comparison, but I think there's some truth to it. We see that stock ticker continuously providing us with information. We keep seeing all those planes on the radar wanting to come in for a landing.

In this regard I remember the movie "Twister" of some years ago, with its graphic images of cows, cars, fencing, trees—all being lifted and thrown about in tornadoes. That's the image that I think has some validity; the things coming at us can be radically *different* from one another. Along with that cow, for example, there's an entire billboard that we have to deal with! These are different *kinds* of things, things we wouldn't ordinarily think of in the same context, and that is exactly where the difficulty comes from in our attempts to do our jobs effectively. Dealing with a sobbing employee needing extended time off, for example, is *really* different from ensuring that every machine in your work area is properly guarded. In turn, monitoring and responding to each of these inputs (the sobbing employee and the need to get the guarding on the machines) is really different from creating and updating financial spreadsheets.

Here is another comparison from the last chapter, a metaphor, to help us get our heads around this concept. The comparison, remember, is that every day each of us has to climb into our respective cockpit, get out the preflight checklist, look at our instruments, and take off. Each of us is a unique processing system, handling or processing the various inputs that approach us in flight—and sometimes before we've even lifted off.

The processing starts early. From the moment you walk in the door in the morning, you're processing your respective inputs: greetings from employees, notes left from the evening shift, emails, voice mail, telephone calls, deliveries, customers, regulators, and whatever electronic or hand-written "to-dos" you've given yourself for the day.

All of these inputs reflect the beans lying along the field (or from part way across the field—hopefully many of them are making progress). The inputs are pleas to "Move *me* today!" Some of the inputs won't come from immediate, external sources such as phone calls or emails. Rather, some will come from your thought life that we described in the last chapter; they will be things that you remember or half-remember that you're supposed to do. They keep cascading by on that stock ticker.

You work within a physical environment in which you carry out your human processing. This would be the building you work in (or field or job site), your office, your desk, your computer, whatever electronic messaging devices you use, your telephone, equipment dedicated to your specific function, and the people who help you carry out your responsibilities. Inputs can and do come from all of these sources, often simultaneously. On that ticker, they cluster in the dimensions we identified earlier, such as people, money, operations, service, planning, compliance, technology and risk.

Filtering the Inputs

I've been critical so far of managers who can't say clearly what they're doing at a given moment in their day. I've been critical of Esther in our first chapter for letting Sarah mistreat my daughter and me at the Caremart jewelry counter. I've said that you as a manager must become aware of and proficient in dealing with *all* of the responsibilities that you've been given. The copilot, remember, can't say to herself, "I don't think I'm going to pay attention to the fuel gauge on this flight."

A seeming paradox is, how can you be this effective responder to *all* the issues that come at you on a moment-to-moment basis? Without, that is, becoming simply the "catcher" I described in Chapter Three?

When we arrive at work in the morning, we may know by plan, intuition and/or urgency which inputs to process, which to lay aside, and perhaps which to ignore completely. But if my main idea in this book is true, that we as managers aren't dealing effectively enough with *all* the responsibilities we've been given, then maybe some fine adjustments to our filtering capacity are in order. This is the very core of "Managing on Purpose."

The basic concept behind any kind of filter is that not everything gets through. As we think about your role as manager, about you as a processor of inputs, we need to design a filtering process for you. Here's one metaphorical filter design that could prove helpful to us.

Imagine a large diameter pipe. You need to react to—intercept—everything coming down the pipe (these will be all the inputs we just spoke of). Coming down the pipe from "upstream" of you are all these inputs vying for your attention on any given day. Before these inputs reach you, there is a slot in the pipe into which you can slide a filtering device. Sections of pipe have flanges into which you could insert such a filtering device.

Stay with me here! This filtering device is made of flexible plate material and has holes of varying sizes, and the holes have screens. The plate material is malleable, which allows screen size to flex or adjust as directed. For simplicity's sake, we're going to call these holes or openings "screens" from this point forward. Imagine that you can adjust both the size of the screen (like the aperture of a camera), and the gauge or mesh of the screens—the actual openings in the screen that the inputs try to squeeze through.

So the filter basically is this big circle, with a variety of screens inside of it, each of which you can control in the manner just described. Is that clear? Good. One large pipe bringing inputs to you; smaller, flexible screens (in terms of their diameters); plate material adjusts to accommodate screen size; mesh sizes adjust to control "permeability"—that which is allowed to squeeze through. Check. Before your work day even starts, you slide this filter into its slot in the pipe. This filter might be your "Monday" filter.

A Manager's Filter (Monday)

Remember the earlier rule about filters: not everything gets through. If you haven't set up a screen for something, and decided how much you're going to let through it (by controlling both the diameter of the filter and the gauge/mesh), it's going to slop up against the filter plate and be forced to backwash down through the divert line into the holding tank. And no, I don't know what your holding tank looks like. Mine is my inbox. And yes, there are a pile of inputs sitting there as I write this, waiting for me to process them! Your non-priority inputs could divert to an email folder or a calendar—hard copy or electronic.

With our Monday filter on the previous page, you see what you've decided to let through that day. Note that we do allow you to "catch" some things. We need to allow space for a SCREAMING CRISIS to get through, but notice that we've limited the size of the screen it has to pass through. We can even dial down the gauge of the screen, and further limit the size of the crisis we elect to deal with.

As we said in the last chapter, a "dashboard" can be any device you have for identifying and monitoring inputs: it can be a paper and pencil to-do list or entries you put in your computer's calendar (which will "tweak" you to attend to a given area of responsibility). When the planned volume of inputs has been processed, you change their status from "To Do" to "Done," and, to continue the metaphor, the alarm on the dashboard goes out—just as when you put fuel in the tank, the "Low Fuel Level" indicator goes out.

Subsequent chapters of this book deal with specific screens in your filter. Those chapters are dedicated to helping you deal as effectively as possible with the people screens, the financial screens, the compliance screens, and so on. You'll have to decide how many screens your filter has, what size they are, how fine the gauge will be in each, and so on. You have to let everything through the screens you've elected to manage on a given day, and you need to manage both screen size and gauge/mesh carefully. Remember you can flex the size of the screens. When Captain Sullenberger saw the condition of his airplane on that January morning, metaphorically speaking he had to flex the SCREAMING CRISIS screen to the limits of its diameter, closing off everything else on the filter.

Let's put this in non-metaphorical language. Say you've decided to deal with some personnel issues that you've been avoiding. You set up your filter accordingly, with a reasonably sized people screen. You may have several "problem children" in your department. If they could, all of these might like to talk to you about an issue on any given day, but you set the screen size to let only two or three through on our Monday in question. The size screen you've selected allows you time to give some personal attention to the several people you've identified.

Only you can do effective filter design and operation. We've already made a beginning here, by suggesting what some screens in a filter can be. Your design will have to guide you on the nature, number and size of the screens that will be in operation on any given day. I know you know this, but you can't keep diverting things to that holding tank indefinitely! While we try to aerate that tank, you know what happens to things that are allowed to stay there too long.

Some of you may realize that this filter analogy is not far-fetched. In process industries, operators watch control screens that show them the status of variables on a moment-to-moment basis. They're looking at variables such as flow, temperature, pressure, consistency, level, and so on. They do exactly what I described above, responding to indicators, gauges and alarms that feed them process information (such as flow, temperature, consistency, level and pressure), sometimes making appropriate adjustments to process set points (for desired flow rate, temperature, consistency level and pressure) that will yield optimum results for the process. That's you: installing those screens, changing diameters as the process requires, monitoring that mesh gauge. That's you limiting the stocks you'll monitor on that ticker.

To return to your own filter design, again using non-metaphorical language, how are you going to decide what is most important to you each day? What will you give highest priority to?

Determining Importance

Within the parameters I've set (eventually you need to screen virtually everything), how large do you make the various screens? If I were an advice-giving person, I would start with creating sizeable screens for those areas that I've been given specific responsibility for. In other words, if I supervise an assembly line, and I'm evaluated on how many widgets my department assembles in a given shift, then I want to pay a lot of attention to any issue coming my way that affects the widget count. If one input I get first thing in the morning is a note saying "The main belt drive for the assembly line went down at 3:30 a.m.—status unknown," that's for sure an input I want to process. So, a large filter screen for "Widget Assembly," and I'll want large gauge/mesh on that screen as well.

If I may be allowed a bias, as indicated above I would suggest a similar-sized screen in the filter for people issues. You can't, after all, assemble widgets without your people. So if inputs in the morning suggest that people are having difficulty of one kind or another—personality conflicts, illnesses, FMLA application forms to process—then you need large screen capacity to handle them.

In a sense this is the same category, but you realize that you are responsible for the safety of your people, right? If there is a hazard in your workplace that you know about and you ignore it, and someone gets hurt because of that hazard, do you know that you could be looking at a fine and potential jail time? Yes to both of the latter: fine and jail time. For this reason, "Safety" should warrant an expansive screen on your filter. Coarse mesh vs. fine mesh. Don't divert those safety inputs, and, if you do, don't let them linger in the holding tank. OSHA pays a lot of attention to this concept called "Management knew or should have known."

Timing is crucial for filter design and operation. What if your organization is in a terrible cash crunch? If it is, and you've already designed your filter with what you perceive to be the proper size and number of screens, you may need to go back to the drawing board. When cash is tight, any input coming through the door concerning money needs to be ushered to your attention as quickly as possible. This is what I meant above when I referred to filter "adjustment."

We'll look more carefully at filter screens—management priorities—in the next chapter.

For Further Consideration

1. Do you agree that management is basically the same, regardless of the kind of business or organization involved? For example, does a pastor need the same knowledge and skill sets as a construction foreman?
2. Is the description in this chapter of you as a processing system fairly accurate? Do you engage in input processing activity as it's described? If it's different, how is it different?
3. Does the image of "things coming at you" describe how you see your responsibilities in the workplace? How so? If not, how would you describe the way your tasks appear to you, and the way you handle them?
4. Do you agree that it's both practical and advisable to "filter" the inputs that approach you on a daily basis? How would you describe your current practice in this area?

5. Does the specific analogy of the pipeline bringing inputs to you work?—does it help you visualize those inputs? If the analogy is inaccurate, can you think of one that's more helpful in describing your particular situation? Remember those air traffic controllers from the last chapter. They literally have dozens of inputs (planes) "coming at them," and they can't afford to ignore any of them. See if you can think of two or three additional analogies or images that more nearly match the "operating reality" of your position.

6. Look at the schematic of a typical filter. If you described a filter like this for yourself, would the screens be the same? The same kinds, and of a similar size? On a piece of paper, draw your own filter, and explain why the screens are the size they are (that is, why do they deserve/require the degree of priority you assign to them?).

7. One screen shown on our sample filter diverts inputs to a holding tank. Do you have ways of diverting any of the inputs that seemingly require your specific attention? Where can you send them? One quick example could be an employee having a question about his/her benefit program. To whom or what would you divert that input?

6 PRIORITIES

Direction

In making my point in the last chapter about the multiple dimensions of a manager's job, I understand that I oversimplify. I do understand that each day on the job isn't spent in the eye of a hurricane, that there is often peace and calm, characterized by the orderly completion of predictable tasks. When it comes to prioritizing inputs on the job, each of us gets at least some direction. *Our* managers provide directions as to what we should do—on a given day, month, or over the course of a year or longer. Mainly, these concern the central function that we are hired to perform.

You get this, right? If you are a sales manager in a car dealership, your boss expects you to see that a lot of cars get sold. If you're a construction foreman, your boss expects the project you're working on to get done on schedule and within budget. If you're a jewelry department manager, your boss expects you to see that a lot of watches get sold, and that customers get treated well.

If we're fortunate, these responsibilities are clarified for us in job descriptions. While most companies and organizations understand the importance of job descriptions, there are still some that don't. Even if your duties and responsibilities aren't formalized in a job description, your boss will give you at least the basic outline of what you're supposed to do and how you're supposed to do it. These basic functions will comprise the largest screens on your input filter, and your success at managing them plays the largest role in upper management's assessment of you (and of course the more positive that assessment, the more likely you are to be rewarded in terms of salary and other "perks" in your organization).

You'll note on the sample filter in the last chapter that one filter screen is labeled "Annual Goals." The direction you get in most organizations will include these. Often managers meet with their direct reports at the end of the year (calendar or fiscal), and ask them to identify goals for the coming year, or however long the performance cycle is.

These goals can be to achieve cost reductions in certain areas; to attain higher scores on employee attitude surveys; to decrease employee turnover; to improve a relationship (e.g. a production manager may not get along as well as he or she should with the environmental manager); to attain a certification; to explore a technology; and so on. In a given performance cycle, you'll perhaps be asked to key in on maybe four-to-six goals.

These goals are important for a variety of reasons. They should keep you focused on key areas of your performance you want to improve, and they can have an additional benefit in that the achievement of them is usually tied to a salary increase. Thus you need to design your filter with ample opportunity for these annual goal inputs to get through. You may see as well that there can be overlap among the screens in your filter. As you see in the sample Monday filter of the last chapter, there's an existing screen for Safety that should always be active. Another screen is for Annual Goals, one of which could be to *improve* safety. This simply allows you to process safety inputs in two ways, which, in our view, increases the likelihood that safety performance overall will improve.

Organization Goals

Enlightened organizations have a vision, mission, and values that guide them in the course of their day-to-day, month-to-month and year-to-year activities. The vision describes what the organization strives to be, the mission how it intends to achieve the vision, and values are the bedrock beliefs that undergird both vision and mission.

You may recall the Tylenol scare of years ago, when contaminants were found in some Tylenol containers. In the face of this Johnson & Johnson (the company that makes Tylenol) could have responded in a number of ways (e.g., mounting a media campaign to minimize the effects, in general doing whatever it felt necessary to control the damage to its image and potential profits). It didn't do that. It took all the containers off of all the store shelves in all the stores, until it had isolated the problem and taken measures to ensure that the contamination that had occurred wouldn't occur again.

These actions were consistent with its vision, mission and values: to be a company that customers could trust absolutely, that had the protocols in place to ensure customer safety, and that valued customer safety before short term profits.

You will be fortunate if you find yourself in such an organization. You'll be fortunate not just to experience the warm feelings generated by examples such as the one above. Your good fortune will also come in the form of the overall, consistent direction provided by your organization's vision, mission and values. These will guide you in moment-to-moment activity during the course of your day. We think, for example, of Toyota assembly lines, in which individual employees are empowered to shut down assembly lines when they feel something they see might compromise quality. On those employee and supervisor filters, in other words, is an enormous opening for Quality.

Organizations clearly operate with filters too, and the Johnson & Johnson and Toyota values described here are indicative of how they want their employees—managers and hourly employees alike—to filter and respond to inputs. As I said a moment ago, we are blessed when we have this kind of filtering guidance from above us.

Being Proactive

The examples above describe an ideal, in terms of organizations communicating to their people what they are to do and how they are to do it. In other words, your superiors should hand you your filter with its screens already sized (and meshed) to specification, say "Here, slide this in," then go on their way, satisfied that the inputs coming toward you on a given day will be processed correctly.

I need to clarify something at this point about our filter metaphor. Again, the basic idea I've asked you to consider is your need to exert control over your responsibilities in the organization. You need to see and respond to whatever comes down that pipe at you—hence the idea of adjustable screens and mesh size. You need to design a way to deal with inputs in a reliable and organized way. Here is the critical point: you decide in advance what you're going to look for, and in the process de-emphasize whatever noise may try to distract you during a given day. If a given screen isn't in place in the filter, guess what? You're right; related inputs go straight through the diverting line to the holding tank.

When you engage in this kind of before-the-fact activity, you really go from defense, as it were, to offense. "Catching" and creating occur in close proximity to one another. You really do "process" inputs, not simply pass them through. You are, to some degree, damming up the stream. The "stream" of inputs passing through you changes as it does so. Because of the priorities you've identified and the processing operations you're able to control, you make something new out of them.

Say, for example, you install and expand your Safety screen on a given day. With that in place, you come across power cords on a manufacturing floor that have been carelessly laid across walkways. This is an input that you need to filter and process. You do, seeing that the cords are properly taped down. Perhaps your Employee Relations screen is dialed in on that same day. An employee needs a review; you give the employee that review.

Input processing thus appears in its true light: at its center it is proactive. It is a process of selecting and prioritizing before the workday even starts—through your identifying of what you choose to filter/process on a given day, and how much of each "stream" you will tackle on the day in question. This all occurs in the process of sizing and installing the filters that we described in the last chapter.

System Issues

As mentioned earlier, when everything functions as it should, vision, mission and values "cascade" through the organization, and individual contributors on the shop or retail floor become the brains, heart, hands and feet of those at the very top of the organization. Everything in the organization is processed in the manner prescribed from the very top. Everyone, as it were, is singing from the same sheet of music.

However, as you are well aware, stuff happens. Disconnects develop. People don't get the memos. Worse, memos are never written in the first place. Elements and functions in the organization, as Rummler and Brache put it, exist in their own "siloes." People in these siloes can come to care more about how their individual function fares day-to-day than they do about the organization as a whole. Relationships among the "siloed" departments deteriorate.

When I say "System Issues" I mean the individual procedures, processes, facilities and technologies operating within organizations. These system considerations collectively comprise how the organization accomplishes or fails to accomplish work. Unfortunately, over time people and departments can come to work at cross purposes, with the result being not a "well-oiled machine," but something far less efficient, productive and profitable. Instead of inter-connected, dependent functions interacting seamlessly and harmoniously with one another, we get siloes. Sometimes, siloes with thick walls.

You have a role to play in seeing that this doesn't happen. In Chapter Seventeen, on Service, I make the point that service should be a primary mindset or frame of reference for everyone in the organization. It is, after all, one organization. I'm tempted again to talk about bee hives and ant hills, about commonality, intention and overall purpose. Everyone in the organization is supposed to work in a concerted, proactive way to move the *entire organization* forward.

A role you have is to pay attention to is those white spaces on the organization chart. Be ready to recognize and process inputs that indicate that those spaces are getting wider instead of narrower—that departments or functions are working against one another versus working together (i.e., that silo walls are thickening). To switch metaphors for a moment, you need to make sure that this dimension of your job stays on your radar screen. Build into your daily agenda (your filter) "Interdepartmental Cooperation," and identify things you can do to promote that. And don't be a Lone Ranger in that effort. Look at work processes, at work flow. Enlist other departments to work with you on those "As Is" process maps, then on the "Should Be" maps. Make this a priority.

The quality movement understood the need for this as a priority, setting us to work on those process maps, with some success. Getting us to do those fishbone diagrams. In organizations I was a part of, however, the effort could devolve into something sterile and mechanistic, especially if enthusiastic support for the effort wasn't forthcoming from the top of the organization. In the absence of that, the siloes can resume their earlier shapes, and work processes suffer proportionately.

<u>A Way Forward</u>

In the ideal organization, your daily choices as a manager can be pretty clear. As we said earlier, your filter can be pretty much configured for you. But as we know, this is rarely the case. You may see little direction from above. You may see people and departments working at cross purposes, even *contradictory* purposes. You may see all kinds of obstacles preventing you from being the manager you'd like to be—the one you know you *could* be if conditions were different.

What are you to do?

In an environment like this one, one in which little filter guidance is provided, you have to, as it were, take the filter by the horns and design it, build it and operate it yourself. And no, you don't do this at your peril. You do this to perform at a higher level, bringing greater satisfaction and better nightly sleep to yourself—and improved performance to your department and the organization as a whole.

Put most simply, operating as best you can on the basis of organization goals and priorities, and on the basis of what you understand your individual functional responsibilities to be (assembling those widgets or selling the watches), you tell your organization what you're going to do.

Let's say that again. *You tell your organization what you're going to do*. You show them your filter with its representative screens and the gauge/mesh you recommend for each. There are a number of ways to do this. One of the best I've found is in Gerber's *The E-Myth Revisited*. What Gerber advises us to do is write what he calls a Position Agreement. A Position Agreement is what it says it is—you can see an example on the next page.

A FRAMEWORK FOR GUIDING SUCCESS IN THE WORKPLACE

ANY COMPANY LLC

Position Agreement Form

This *Position Agreement Form* is to be completed after an annual review with the employee of his/her Job Description. Following that review, there should be several areas in which the employee can set goals for the coming year—in terms of helping with process improvements; in terms of job duties and responsibilities; and/or in terms one or more of the company's performance criteria. The focus areas need not be in the equal proportions shown below, nor must there be six of them in any given year. For example, an employee may choose to focus all his/her efforts toward several of the performance criteria, and he/she may choose to focus on just three of those. However they are distributed, each employee should include at least three goals for the year.

Position:_____

Reports to:_____

Incumbent:_____

In _____ (Year) , the incumbent is accountable for the following:

Process Improvement Goal 1:
Process Improvement Goal 2:
Job Duty/Responsibility Goal 1:
Job Duty/Responsibility Goal 2:
Performance Criterion Goal 1:
Performance Criterion Goal 2:

_____   _____
Employee Signature   Date

_____   _____
Manager/Supervisor Signature   Date

Upper management of course is advised to ask for these from everyone—how else will it know what's happening, or what should be happening, on a moment-to-moment basis? Remember our "Same old same old" manager from Chapter Three? I guess he or she could write "Same old same old" in each box of the *Agreement*, but I just don't think that's going to suffice.

Perhaps more importantly, especially if you find yourself in an organization that is less than clear in its priorities, you tell *yourself* what you're going to do. You give yourself direction, complete with specific things you'll accomplish and when you'll accomplish them. The resulting screens will filter out the unproductive "noise" that comes at you every day. You'll send products downstream that you can be proud of.

Vision, Mission and Values

There's an old saying that if you don't stand for something, you'll fall for anything. Think about this before committing (in writing) to the items you put on your *Agreement* form. Some of those, remember, will be fairly cut and dried, especially those that pertain to your primary function. You'll commit to various sales, production, profit, safety and employee relations goals.

But if your organization doesn't have a vision, mission, and values for you to conform to, your Agreement/Filter should be informed by your own vision, mission, and values. Your priorities, in other words, should reflect the kind of person and the kind of manager you want to be. As you commit to filter screens and sizes, and then live them moment to moment in your workplace, you become an army of one acting in their behalf. You become what might be called a Guerilla in the Midst (yes, that is my own idea). There is pride and satisfaction in that.

What happens in organizations in which this occurs is that they become managed from the bottom up. Even when managers lack the kind of formal processes and tools we're talking about (e.g. the Position Agreements), we've all known individual managers whose character, ethics and operating manner are so well known that their basic qualities and methods tend to percolate up in the organization.

Managers at all levels see how Joe is doing things. They see the response from his people and the concrete results he's getting, and they want to do likewise. Even though they may lack his actual ethics and character—and perhaps his operating know-how—they can act as if they have them. And if they act as if they have them long enough, guess what? They will eventually "hard wire" themselves into these people, and what has been pretend becomes integral—it becomes real.

For Further Consideration

1. This chapter suggests that the "main thing" each of us as a manager is responsible for is usually pretty clear (it's essentially what we were hired to carry out). What is this in your case? How satisfied are you with your execution of this primary responsibility? If you could change

something that affects your success in dealing with it, what would it be?

2. Describe the way your organization sets goals—in both "macro" (organization-wide) and "micro" (department-specific) ways. If you could change anything in the current system, what would it be? Why?

3. If you are the owner/manager of a small business, do you set goals? How are these goals articulated to others in the organization? What incentives are in place for your people when they achieve or surpass their goals?

4. Do you think the example cited in this chapter, of Johnson & Johnson and the way the company handled the Tylenol scare, is typical of many organizations? Do many organizations in your experience have this kind of identity? What can keep an organization from developing such a "personality" in the marketplace? What can you do to help your organization develop one?—or change the one that currently exists?

5. Do you understand the concept of "silos" in organizations—departments that essentially wall themselves off from one another? If so, what are some consequences you've seen of this? If you could change that so-called silo mentality, how would you?

6. Rummler and Brache say that bad systems defeat superior performers every time. Can you think of examples of such systems in your working life? What were the eventual consequences? Have you seen individual "heroes" prevail against such systems? How did they do it?

7. Can you explain in your own words how the process of filtering inputs transforms them—and in the process, changes you from "catcher" to creator?

8. If you lack specific direction in your working life, do you think it feasible to draft a Position Agreement such as the sample offered in this chapter? Why/why not? What could keep you from becoming a Guerilla in the Midst?

This is the end of Part I. Now it's time to look at all the dimensions of your job, and see how we can prepare you to execute your responsibilities successfully in each of them.

PART II: APPLICATIONS

7 THE POTENTIAL FOR CHANGE

<u>Old Managers, New Tricks?</u>

You know what happened to the Titanic, right? People on the ship saw the iceberg, but they couldn't change course in time. The ship scraped the iceberg, a huge gash got ripped in its side, eventually causing flooding to occur in supposedly water-tight compartments. Enough of those compartments filled and the ship sank.

In this chapter we need to talk about changing course. Or not. Maybe you're just reading this book for entertainment; maybe you're satisfied with how things are going for you as a manager. But if you realize now that there are some parts of your job that you need to take second and third looks at, that your bean-moving hasn't been as rapid and effective as you'd like it to be, then we run headlong into the concept of change. If you're to take maximum advantage of the next part of this book, which deals with concrete suggestions for managing the major dimensions of your job, then you need to stop here and think about how you react to the concept of change.

I'll give away my bias right away. Anyone can change. Anyone can change *dramatically*. So if you're even tempted to say, "I could never do it that way," dispose of that thought immediately. If you're in a modern workplace, you've already had to change in many important ways (revisit Chapter Two, "How Are We Doing?"). But people can get stuck, so even if you've embraced the concepts that we've studied so far, getting your filter in place and defining and acting on your priorities, you still may harbor some doubts about whether you can make the changes needed to perform more effectively.

Change Management 101

In earlier chapters we dealt with the concept of seeing. If you can't "see" something, it's hard to move forward and be successful. Consider Helen Keller. Helen Keller of course couldn't see or hear. She had to move out of the safe cocoon of family life, in which she'd been comforted and indulged, and placed in the care of a teacher, Annie Sullivan. Annie taught Helen sign language, and her lessons finally "took" in dramatic fashion when she held Helen's hand in a stream of water that Annie was pumping, while signing WATER into Helen's hand. That enabled Helen to "see" what Annie had been trying and trying to get through to her, that things in Helen's world had names. She learned to apply those names, then went on to the dazzling accomplishments she became known for.

Here is something I saw happen when I taught writing. People in writing class approach the task with a lot of baggage. They think they can't do it; they can't "see" themselves doing it successfully. But early on, if you put the emphasis on drafting—on simply accumulating some pages of writing—you see something interesting happen. I remember watching one boy in particular, a high school sophomore, when he was asked to do something with some draft pages he'd written. He got them out of a folder, perhaps six or seven pages total, and, holding them with both hands, stacked and straightened them until they comprised this neat, even pile.

Have you seen that? It's what you do just before you staple a bunch of pages together. You have to get the edges straight or it won't look right. I watched this young man straightening his pages with this satisfied look on his face, as if to say, "I did this."

I would extend that to "I can do this." But first, he had to be made to *see* it.

Installed Bases

"Installed bases" can refer to the actual number of things—heating or computer systems for example—that are actually installed and operating, usually in a given area or among a certain demographic. I've also heard this phrase used to describe a deeply held attitude or belief, and that's the way I'd like you to consider it for a moment.

In this sense an installed base is like a paradigm. Paradigms are our perceptions; they're the way we've come to see something. The current political paradigm, for example, is that Republicans and Democrats can't talk to one another; rather, they need to scream invectives at one another. Some believe that another paradigm is possible, one that might actually get work done for the country.

In the sense I'm using the phrase, for a change to occur we often have to exchange one installed base for another. This is not unlike a machine that uses dyes to stamp out different sizes of products. You have to actually unbolt one dye and replace it with another—which, when I've seen it done, can be quite a cumbersome and labor-intensive process. But the point is you couldn't achieve a different result, producing the new product, unless you took the time and effort to "uninstall" one base and replace it with another.

Those who implement change in organizations sometimes short circuit this phase of the process. They think that whatever the organization is changing to (e.g. a new process or system), can simply be overlaid onto whatever has existed before, and this is rarely true. You have to look first at the base that is installed, acknowledge its service and praise its accomplishments, explain how the new base is in some respects very similar to the old one, *then* proceed with the installation of the new base.

I say all this because you have installed bases as a manager. Through what you read in this book and elsewhere, you're being asked to consider making some changes in the ways you think and act as a manager. I understand that loosening some bolts and perhaps drilling some larger diameter screens (filter, remember?) here and there may take us time and effort, but I'm saying that it can be done. What has served you well over the years is to be applauded, and we certainly don't want to throw any babies out with the bathwater. We don't want you to remove and discard bases that may be perfectly serviceable.

Frame of Reference

The installed bases that I've been talking about, taken together, comprise a frame of reference—I've also referred to this as a mindset. Meaningful change only occurs through significant changes in our frame of reference, our way of seeing and responding to the world. Let's envision for a moment our actual frames of reference. They might look like those below, Frame 1 and Frame 2.

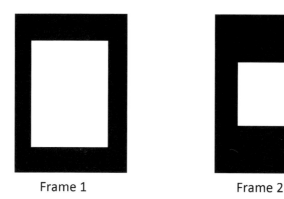

Frame 1   Frame 2

A frame of reference—mindset—consists of the accumulated ideas or paradigms each of us has about life. Usually, the older we get, the "thicker" these frames of reference become, simply because we've had more time to think, and perhaps become more set in our ways. I understand that this is a complete overgeneralization, but I want you to bear with me for a moment.

My idea is that we look out through our frames of reference at the world. If our vision is clouded or blocked by the ideas, attitudes, preconceptions and beliefs that have accumulated over time, my view is that we literally can't "see" as well as we might. Our point of view is restricted to quite a degree.

I had a business associate, for example, who was severely affected by a divorce that had happened many years prior to my meeting her. This event had such a traumatic effect on her—created such a thickening of her frame of reference—that it severely limited her ability to see: to broaden her horizons, so to speak. Everything had to be seen and processed through the dramatically narrowed vision caused by the divorce.

What this suggests to me is that we need to continually monitor our frames of reference. There can be ideas and preconceptions there that are no longer valid, and they effectively block our capacity to see differently—more broadly—and implement change. If you have been managing for quite a long time, maybe your frame of reference has thickened a bit as well. Maybe yours is more like Frame 2 than Frame 1.

If it is, I want you to think about peeling some of it away, trying to make it more like Frame 1. What you will peel away are thoughts about yourself that are no longer valid, especially those that sound like "I can't do this." I've had those, for example, in connection with my ability to understand technology. I've had similar ones with math. Neither has proven to be true; I am becoming more comfortable with technology, and I am also a "numbers guy" for my clients. It can be done.

Remember, you're supposed to be this agile person now. It's hard to be agile when you're carrying this too-thick frame of reference around with you. The narrower the frame, the easier inputs and outputs can flow back and forth, and that's what they need to do in the modern workplace. Do this. Draw your frame of reference. Maybe it will be thick like Frame 2. Once you've drawn it, actually write in what the "thickening agents" are—ideas, prejudices, preferences, judgments—that may no longer be valid. Once you've written those in, draw lines through all the ones you're going to get rid of, and re-draw your frame. Maybe it will look more like this. This is Frame 3—the "New You"!

Frame 3

Here is the thing. To be as agile as we're required to be, we need, as individual human beings, to be as "transparent" as we can be. This means our past experience has to be available to us, and we also need to keep the "lens" of our perceiving capacity wide open. We can't "screen" off ideas, people and possibilities. We can't limit ourselves.

Phillip Hunsaker has an interesting way of describing the change process in his *Training in Management Skills*. To accomplish change (and I'm looking at this now in the context of changing our perceptions of ourselves as managers), he says we need to be clear about what the current state of something is (this happened when I asked you to draw your existing frame of reference); what a transitional state might look like (this is you peeling away the unprofitable ideas about yourself); and what a new state might look like (this is the new, transparent, agile you shown in Frame 3).

Hunsaker refers to this as unfreezing, changing, and refreezing. I'm not sure about the "freezing" part, because it sounds like replacing one kind of rigidity with another, but I do like the idea that we need to, in effect, take the hammer to ourselves! We need to "break up" whatever may be freezing us in place, reconfigure ourselves, then proceed in a new, healthier way.

A Blizzard of Change

You realize, of course, that I'm not the only one talking about the need for change. For at least the last several decades, we've heard about the new workplace in America, one characterized by the rapidity of change, and once again, the need for manager agility in the face of that change. Tom

Peters in *Thriving on Chaos*[1] made this point, talking about the need for shared leadership—about managers being able to relinquish control of traditional functions and place them at least in part in the hands of empowered teams. This has to involve a considerable narrowing of a traditional management frame of reference.

Similarly, in 1995 Judith Bardwick in *Danger in the Comfort Zone*[2] talked about the need to overcome what she called the "Entitlement Habit," which creates in managers and employees alike an unsustainable acceptance of the status quo. Rather than being accommodating "families" of employees, Bardwick wants us to create "earning cultures," ones that are ". . .results oriented so that all activities move the rock. That means everything that people do is *purposeful;* their actions make a difference. They don't put energy or time into garbage. Garbage is all the stuff that people do that uses up resources but doesn't make a difference." (p. 200) For this to work, clearly managers need full awareness of what their various purposes are, along with the knowledge, skill and ability to achieve them.

In what I refer to here as a "blizzard of change," managers indeed need to flee from "same old same old." Bruce Avolio, Bernard Bass and others have articulated what they call "Full Range Leadership," which describes a range of responses (ways to process and respond to inputs), that we as managers need to absorb and draw from (read example cases in their *Developing Potential Across a Full Range of Leadership*[3], which provides case studies of leaders employing "full range" thoughts and actions in the real workplace; these are also covered in Chapter Eighteen, *Leading*). I mention this here to underscore my main point in this chapter, which is that you will of necessity need to learn more agile ways to think and act—paring down what can be that too-thick frame of reference.

I talked about management and value in Chapter Three, emphasizing that all of us as managers, as assets in our organizations, need to demonstrate concrete, measurable value. Demonstrating this value in the rapidly changing workplace is the subject of *Competing Values Leadership: Creating Value in Organizations* by Cameron, Quinn and DeGraff[4].

In this book the authors make clear that there is no *one* dimension in organizations in which managers must be proficient, but in fact there are several. In their words, we need to be able to survive and flourish in organizational dimensions characterized by qualities such as collaboration (these qualities are often embodied in the HR people); creativity (these by the colorful zanies in research and development); control (these are hugely important to accountants); and competition (these appear typically in Type A managers and sales people). As managers we need to not only recognize these different value "quadrants," but develop the ability to demonstrate value along diagonals *between* various quadrants, exhibiting qualities such as "caring confrontation," "practical vision," and "autonomous engagement." Transparency, flexibility, agility. That's us.

Current State Revisited

Change is the air we breathe in our businesses and organizations. In light of this, how can we not adopt a willingness to change?—in fact, to become change agents ourselves? Remember, as managers we are to *facilitate work*, and we can't do that by relying on an image, a perception of the workplace itself and of ourselves as managers that is rigid and outmoded.

Now, this may be the most important thing I've said in these first several chapters: I wouldn't have felt compelled to write this book in the first place if, perhaps as a result of thinking embodied in books such as those just cited, managers were "getting it."

But too many managers are simply not getting it.

In all my working life, starting back way more decades than I'll reveal, I've seen the same rigidity, the same reliance on management approaches that are wrong-headed and counter-productive. That was true decades ago, and when I looked last week, it's still true. And it would be one thing if work could proceed smoothly and positive results be achieved through what we'll call traditional approaches, but too often they can't be.

What I'm calling traditional approaches often focus on the manager, rather than the people and processes being managed. If what we do in the workplace flows from this kind of "me first" orientation, we usually get the results we deserve. As managers we need to be contributing cogs in the "well-oiled machine," not wrenches thrown into the gears of that machine.

The traditional approaches persist in part because we resist change. We like stability. We like to know what to expect. Sure this thick frame of reference is heavy, but we're used to it! But to cite a really time-worn idea, the problem is that all we can really be sure of in the workplace today is change itself. In light of this, we need to make ourselves into the responsive entities that can handle and even thrive on that change.

A seeming paradox is that our employees require stability and consistency of us. Is that possible? I sure think so. What can remain stable is the processing apparatus itself (that's you), a "machine" if you will that employees can rely on to hear them (all of them, including the ones with the body art) clearly and respond fairly. You can be someone who, because of your filter's sizeable people screen, complemented by the new thinness in that frame of reference, welcomes their concerns, celebrates their successes, and perhaps most importantly, facilitates their work moment-by-moment, hour-by-hour.

You do need to be flexible. You need to understand this "blizzard of change" as the environment you live in. You need to know that only by being willing to change *yourself* can you be a positive, productive force within that environment.

For Further Consideration

1. Do you agree that fundamental change is possible for human beings? What is the most striking change you've ever seen in an individual? What were the factors contributing to the change?—that made it possible?

2. Have you ever helped someone "see" a task or concept in such a way that he or she had a so-called "Eureka" moment? The person all of a sudden "got it"? How did you achieve the breakthrough? What, if anything, keeps us from replicating those kinds of moments?

3. How does the frame of reference idea strike you? List again those ideas and preconceptions you "weeded out" of your frame of reference in this chapter.

4. Do you get the idea of installed bases? Do you have employees whose existing installed bases make them difficult to manage? How would you describe them (the installed bases)? How have you tried to "uninstall" those bases, and put new ones in place? What lessons have you learned in the process?

5. Do you perceive yourself as one who handles change well? Give some examples of changes that have gone well for you, and some that you may still be struggling with—especially in your working life as a manager.

6. While it's touched on only briefly in this chapter, can you see different qualities or emphases operating in different parts of your organization?—are the sales people, for example, in synch with maintenance people, and vice-versa? Is everyone at least singing the same hymn, perhaps as tenors, altos and sopranos—but at least the

same song? If not, what management qualities do you think it would take to change these dynamics, to bridge the gaps?

7. Do you agree with the position taken in this chapter, that we resist change—especially perhaps in the way we carry out our responsibilities as managers? Why/why not?

Notes

1. Peters, Tom. *Thriving on Chaos: Handbook for a Management Revolution*. New York: Knopf. 1987. Print.
2. Bardwick, Judith M. *Danger in the Comfort Zone*. New York: AMACOM, 1995. Print.
3. Avolio, Bruce J., and Bass, Bernard M. *Developing Potential Across a Full Range of Leadership*. Mahwah, New Jersey: Lawrence Erlbaum Associates, Inc. 2002. Print.
4. Cameron, Kim S., DeGraff, Jeff, and Quinn, Robert E. *Competing Values Leadership: Creating Value in Organizations*. Northhampton, Massachusetts: Edward Elgar Publishing, Inc. 2006. Print.

8 PEOPLE AS PRIORITY

<u>The Highest Priority</u>

You may have heard companies espouse the idea that "people are our highest priority." People should be the highest priority. I understand that robots are doing lots of the work on assembly lines; I understand as well that expanding proportions of work are being handled by computers. But for our foreseeable future, we still need people, and we still need to manage them effectively.

I hope that isn't just the most trite thing you've ever heard. I hope you don't respond "Everybody knows that." I say this because we either don't know it, or we exemplify the idea that "To know and not do is not to know." Because what I've seen over and over again (and remember, this was true as of last week) many of us don't seem to get it. We don't seem to understand the value of our people.

Just from a nuts and bolts, dollars and cents perspective, we need to optimize the contributions of each person in the organization. Remember the new bulldozer in the parking lot from Chapter Three. Each person in an organization has similar potential to deliver enormous value. Think about the people in your department or your company, and ask yourself what percentage of potential value you're receiving from each of them.

What's your number? Sixty percent? Seventy? When the experts look at this, they chart an upward movement on a graph, starting from when an employee is hired, through the period when he/she is being trained, and through the time when he/she becomes a satisfactory performer (i.e., knowing enough and being willing enough to carry out his/her responsibilities). Always, above that "optimization line," there is the potential for the employee to deliver more in the way of performance—to deliver *discretionary* effort.

The line on the graph often rises quickly as the employee learns the basics of the job, then the ascent becomes more gradual as the complexities of the job are encountered and eventually mastered. What can happen then is a plateau is reached, and the upward movement of additional mastery and proficiency—and I would say effort—level out. Heaven forbid that the line would start back down, but it often does. We want our employees' "Potential Realized" percentage to be high. Ninety percent? A hundred? Why not?

Seeing Employees in a Different Light

As I write this, much is being made in management literature of employee engagement. A library of material exists to help us do those things that will in turn help our employees engage more fully with their specific responsibilities and with the purposes of the organization as a whole. Since we've become so lean and mean, we really need the people we still have to take their responsibilities and run with them.

Instead of delving deeply into the pure science of employee engagement, I want you to think about how you "see" the people who work for you. Remember, our whole point in this book is to get you to see your job as a manager "all of a piece," managing all the inputs that comprise your management responsibility. The people screen of your filter, as we saw in our model in Chapter Five, has to be one of the largest screens. All of the inputs clamoring for your attention do need to be processed through screens of appropriate size according to their relative priority (or temporarily diverted). However, much of the time you need to pay the hardest attention to the inputs coming from your people.

So, how *do* you see your people? This question is more complex than you may realize, because the way you see them affects the way you treat them, the way you "handle" them. In my days as a laborer in the box plant 113 years ago, my foreman Bernie Stopko was fond of saying (this after I'd destroyed another pallet-load of product), "Hall, if you can't run this machine I'll get someone over here who can!"

Let's consider the attitude behind that comment, the "vision" of me as employee that emerges. First of all, he didn't call me "Jim," which kind of hurt my feelings. Now that I think about it, he could have said "Jim my friend. . ." Truly, that would have been a stretch. So he called me by my last name, which had the effect of widening the interpersonal distance between us. Second, there was the serious suggestion that I lacked the wherewithal to operate the machine ("if you can't run this machine"). And finally, I was totally replaceable ("I'll get someone over here who can").

Do you know where the term "hands" comes from? As in "farmhand," or "All hands on deck," or "We need to find a hired hand"? Originally, it comes from the idea that workers were no more than their hands (and backs); what they were valued for was the volume of work they could produce through the work of their hands. Not as whole people with lives, priorities, and aspirations—they were valued as "hands."

Of course you see what's wrong with this picture. We need more than people's hands (again, in part because we have so few people now); we need to have our people participating with as much of themselves as possible, helping us in as many dimensions of organization life as possible and practicable: planning, creating, solving problems, "going the extra mile." And you know what? Even in my time with Bernie in the box plant, I *wasn't* totally replaceable. In fact, I was *irreplaceable*, in terms of what the plant had invested in me, and in terms of the potential I could have exercised on the company's behalf. Bernie was lucky I didn't walk out on the spot.

Perhaps you gave up "seeing" your people as "hands" long ago, and you are this enlightened being who is fully conscious and aware of everything each one of them brings to the table. If not, we need to make both a screen size and gauge/mesh adjustment to your people filter. In other words, you may need to install a larger diameter screen for your people. As for the mesh size, this is your call, and it will vary with working reality. Sometimes you allow wider spaces, allowing you to do more with fewer people; sometimes you shrink the mesh down, allowing you to do less with a greater number. In non-metaphorical language, sometimes you may need to invest training time with a relatively small number of your people. Other times you may need to attend to administrative matters (new badges? hearing tests? benefits enrollment?) that involve all of them.

Practical Appreciation

Bernie Stopko didn't need to go to sensitivity training in order to "handle" me more effectively. What he needed to do was understand his core function: to get maximum, quality production from me on his shift, and make sure that I'd be back the next day and deliver that production again. The question becomes, which tactic—which method of bean pushing—would have worked better in his dealings with me? The fear did work pretty well, in that I needed the job and was afraid of losing it. But it's also true that my rather fragile self concept didn't benefit from his yelling at me that way. In the years that I worked in the box plant, Bernie did eventually call me "Jim," which I thought was progress.

What Bernie could have done was prepare me better to do that particular job (or asked someone else to prepare me). Even in those days I wasn't a technologically-oriented person. I didn't understand the machines I worked on (corrugators, presses, stitchers, gluers); I was scared of them. Had anyone in the plant taken the time to teach me some basics about those machines, I'm sure I would have performed better. Had anyone ever told me how important my contribution was, I would have performed better. Had Bernie shown some interest in and understanding of me as a separate human being—who knows? I could have been a foreman. Before you can say it, I know—another stretch.

When I say "appreciate our people" I don't mean just being thankful for them, although that is important. A better word may be "understand." And even within the definition of "understand," I don't mean that we have our employees lie on couches and tell us about their childhoods. What I do mean for one thing is that we understand their human needs to be seen as successful in the tasks we assign to them. I didn't want to break the stitcher the day Bernie yelled at me. I wanted to be a good operator. Bernie could have understood my need for training, for more guided practice on the job, and he could have given me some "attaboys" when I did things right. If he wanted to know and understand more things about me as a person, that would have been good too.

So this section is called "Practical Appreciation" for a reason. We can demonstrate a practical, not a warm and fuzzy kind of appreciation. If you attempt the warm and fuzzy approach to bean moving, you probably won't be successful. People tend to hate phoniness and manipulation (often couched in warmth and fuzziness) even more than they hate being yelled at.

Your job is to help your people, to facilitate their performance. Stephen Covey has this image of people hacking their way through a jungle. The workers are those wielding the machetes; the managers (this is you) are busy giving people breaks, teaching people the niceties of hacking with a machete, supplying insect repellant, sharpening machetes, and providing food and water. The leaders, as opposed to the managers, are the ones up in the trees shouting "Wrong jungle!"

Covey has this additional concept he refers to as "emotional bank accounts," and it's a very useful one. When we develop positive relationships with people, we're said to have built up emotional bank accounts with them We have a reserve of good will upon which we can draw. In the normal course of things, this balance remains pretty constant. But, what happens when we do something that leads to a withdrawal— if we mess up with someone, say losing our temper with him or her? If we have no balance of good will built up, such a withdrawal can really hurt the relationship. If we have a lot in the account, on the other hand, the relationship can weather the storm without breaking apart. Think about that. How do these accounts stand with your people?   What kind of balances do you have?

You need to know the answer to that question. Your employees are the absolutely essential ingredients in your department's or your company's ultimate success. You are the one who finds them (HR helps with this), welcomes them, trains them, learns their names and histories, keeps them on track, keeps their machetes sharp, makes them want to come back the next day, and perhaps most importantly, prepares them for positions of greater responsibility within the organization. This is the way you have to come to "see" them and your relationship with them. As we make clear in Chapter Seventeen, which is about service, ultimate success in the workplace is primarily about them, not you.

How Your People See You

Not that you don't have enough responsibility—and enough to worry about—already, but the way your people "see" you is critical. It's the criterion that factors most heavily in the amount and degree of discretionary effort they apply, and it's the criterion that determines in the end how long they stay with the organization. If they "see" you in a less-than-favorable light, their chances of performing at sub-optimal levels, and even leaving the organization, increase. Much depends on the balance in that emotional bank account.

Understand this as well. You may not be fully conscious of how heavily each of your interactions with your people influences them. Even when you don't say anything to someone, the way you look at him or her can affect the quality of his or her hours and days. For this reason you need to look at each of those interactions with great care; you need to turn each one of them into an opportunity to strengthen an employee's commitment to you and your organization.

So your employees' degree of commitment and engagement depends first on how they see you, which in turn depends on what *you* do in your day-to-day interactions with them. Here are some actions on your part that can make their impressions of you positive ones, that place deposits in the account, so to speak.

- Make sure the people screen in your management filter is large in proportion to others (i.e., be open to processing more inputs through that screen than any other). Don't ignore your people and their issues in favor of other, apparently pressing obligations (keep the diameter of that SCREAMING CRISIS screen small).
- Remember who you are to your employees. Your every word, look and gesture are important; there are no neutral actions and interactions.
- Listen to them. Communicate back what you hear; be ready to alter what you've heard based on the feedback they give you.
- Consider finding out how your employees see you. You can simply ask them individually (get some guidance from HR before you do this), or do something more formal such as an attitude survey. Be ready to act on what you learn.
- Keep your word to them (doing otherwise really depletes the account).
- Supply consequences for both positive and negative performance.
- "Clear the deck" (remove barriers) for your people so they can concentrate on tasks at hand.

- Remember that you are there to serve them, and not vice-versa.
- Be yourself (being phony is a major account drainer).
- Demonstrate consistent values, ethics, integrity and character (it's best if these are positive values, ethics, integrity and character).
- Clarify expectations. This is the foundation of every relationship, not just your relationship with your employees.

Communication

I was once blessed to be one of several HR managers for a large, urban manufacturer. The plant was your standard melting pot, with a widely diverse employee population. In my HR capacity I heard and resolved disputes between supervisors and the people who worked for them. What I heard repeatedly from the employees, in talking about their bosses, was that the bosses didn't know how to talk to them.

And in fact, the employees' managers and supervisors often *didn't* know how to talk to their people. The overall diversity in the plant contributed to this. Literally, people spoke different languages. I sometimes had trouble decoding messages sent by my Vietnamese, Filipino and South Asian employees. I would sometimes need to have speakers of these and other languages translate for me. What I could do with these translators, in effect, was substitute their receiving mechanisms for mine. They would "get" the message from its sender, and put it in a language I could understand.

Sometimes other dynamics were in play, primarily cultural ones. Our younger African American employees, for example, placed a high value on respect. Any communication from a supervisor, either through his/her body language or through actual words, that suggested *dis*respect, would be distorted or blocked. Demonstrating respect, in other words, was a key component of knowing how to talk to that particular group of employees.

Dynamics

So I want you to work on your ability to communicate. I want you to increase your ability to empathize with your people; the simplest definition of that is putting yourself in their shoes, understanding "where they're coming from." Often, we have little idea where they're coming from. The way we find out where they're coming from is to pay attention and listen to them. Let's say that together: "Pay attention and listen to them." A phrase you can cultivate and repeat is "What I hear you saying is. . ." Another is, "I can see you have really strong feelings about this. . ." What those kinds of statements communicate is that you understand that everyone does not see things the same way, and you also give them the opportunity to amend what you've heard—as many times as necessary, until you find yourselves on the same page.

Here are some gnarly facts about communication. We often have to rely on words, and words mean different things to different people. Words have both dictionary and "feeling" definitions (the latter means that they can *suggest* different things to different people). The gnarliness of this equation occurs in two ways. First, we configure messages in peculiar ways when we *send* them (e.g., with the terms we use, the length of our sentences, the sound of our voices, the volume of our voices, and with the emotional intensity we attach to them). In short, we mangle our messages with our sending "instruments" when we send them.

And you've already guessed it: we mangle them when we *receive* them in many of the same ways. Because of our receiving apparatus, we don't understand a key term; many thoughts are rushed together too quickly for us to separate and decode them; the person's voice quality is extremely off-putting; his/her expression reminds us too much of our Aunt Edna—all of these factors can keep us from really hearing what someone is trying to convey to us. Hearing someone really takes work. It requires our full attention; it requires that we listen on purpose—to really hear what is being said over all the other noise.

I know; communication is a subject for several books in and of itself. Until we can get to those, widen the diameter of the people screen. Monitor the balances in your accounts; keep them full.

Last Word

The subject of this chapter is so important, and my space to deal with it is so limited. Be proactive and purposeful in your dealings with your people. Talk *with* them, not *at* them. Covey's fifth "effective people" habit is Seek First to

Understand, then to be Understood. That is such good advice, and so opposite to the way that most of us as managers proceed. We want things to be about us; we assume that others are *like* us, and they aren't.

Let me say this one more time. As managers we need to understand—especially in the diverse universe we find ourselves in—that not everyone sees things the way we do. Each of us, all our lives, has been constructing an elaborate world view, a way of "seeing" that is peculiar to us as individuals. This becomes the paradigm or prism through which we see and make sense of our worlds—the frame of reference that we discussed in Chapter Seven. To go all scientific on you, everything is "refracted" through that frame of reference. Your "vision" is wildly different from mine, and wildly different from that of your employees.

Before people will deliver what we ask of them, they need to perceive that we understand them. Start with that. Speak languages that they understand. Do this and people will say of you, "She may have her shortcomings, but she sure knows how to talk to people!"

Covey says on this point that when you and I communicate, if I don't perceive that you understand my *uniqueness*, I won't be receptive to your *influence*. Think about that. It means that a single approach that assumes that people are pretty much the same is just not going to work.

Think about the times that anyone has really "seen" you. Think about how few people really "get" you. Think about how much you appreciate this when it happens. Think about what you're willing to do in friendship for these people.

Don't look for "hands" in your workplace. See and influence separable, unique individuals, all of whom have a great deal to offer.

<u>For Further Consideration</u>

1. What is your answer to the "percent of optimization" question posed at the beginning of this chapter? Do you see people at all levels pushing themselves to higher and higher levels of achievement in your organization? If so, what appears to be driving those efforts? If not, what is keeping them from greater achievement?

2. How are those emotional bank accounts that you have with your people looking? Which, if any, are low? What kind of deposits could you make to get them back to a "safe" level?

3. Generalize if you can about the way you "see" your people. Do you tend to see most of them in the same light, or are you able to see and respond to distinct needs and interests? If not, what keeps you from doing so? Is it perhaps possible to go too far in focusing on people's different needs and aspirations? Explain your answer.

4. In your working life, can you cite some examples of how your superiors "saw" and treated you, in terms of either squelching or optimizing your potential? What lessons are there for you in your current career as a manager?

5. This chapter suggests that employees pick up readily on perceived phoniness and manipulation on the part of

their managers. Do you think this is true? Can you cite examples from your own experience? How does a manager remain "authentic" in dealing with widely diverse employees in the workplace?

6. If you had to speculate, how do you think your people "see" you as their boss? On what do you base your answer? Given this perception, what can you do to either alter or reinforce it?

7. Think about yourself for a moment as both a sender and receiver of messages. What tools do you employ to ensure that your messages are clear, and that they achieve the purposes you have for them? By the same token, how do you rate your capacity as a receiver? What factors can cause static in the messages you receive? What can you do to improve the reception?

8. Explain in your own words the importance of everyone not seeing things the way you do. Isn't this overstated a bit? Isn't there a concrete reality we can all agree and act on? Describe some instances in which you've had to deal with the concept of differing "realities." Were you able to bring them into any kind of congruence or harmony? How did you do it?

9. Think for a moment about your direct reports. Is there one individual in that group who could profit from your seeing him/her in a different light? In other words, is there potential in that individual that is remaining below the surface, and not being utilized to a higher degree in the organization? What might you do to change this situation?

9 MANAGERS AND FINANCE

The Most Sensitive Topic

Preachers don't like to talk about money. Concern over money and the willingness to talk about it play a large role in the health of marriages. As I write this, concern over our country's debt ceiling and other financial issues—especially debt, taxes and spending—has our national government virtually paralyzed. My business clients grow visibly pale when I ask to see their financial records.

Perhaps there's a mystique about money and the way we manage it. If so, a first thing we need to do in our discussions about money is *de*mystify it. Money is a medium; it's a commodity. In your church, family, organization, city government or workplace, you need to develop a willingness to understand money in that way:

- It's not voodoo.
- It should be emotionally neutral.

- We need no innate financial gene in order to understand and work with it successfully.

In our ignorance or even superstition we can give money power over us, and there's no need for us to do this. We need to use money productively instead of being used by it (giving it emotional weight in our lives that it really shouldn't have). Knowledge is critical in this "reclaiming" process, and we'll learn key terms and concepts in this chapter that should help in this effort. I want you to acknowledge this fact right now: regardless of your current job description, regardless of the position you occupy, regardless the purpose of your organization—you are a financial manager. You need to be as expert in this dimension of your job as any other. Agreed? Good.

Facing Financial Facts

My dad might have been the worst financial manager on the planet. Bless his heart, he came of age in the Great Depression in the 1930's doing farm work. He came to understand lack first hand. In a cruel irony, when he left the farm at an early age he went into sales, often working for the rest of his life on straight commission. If you've read Arthur Miller's *Death of a Salesman*, you've read my dad's life story.

As with anything else, my dad's *perception* of something, money in this instance, played an important role in the way he interacted with it. If there's a normal perception of family finance, it includes acquiring enough money to meet basic needs, dispersing it appropriately (paying bills), and saving/investing some for the future.

My dad didn't quite get this. His farm background taught him, "If I plant these seeds, corn will come up, and we'll be able to sell what we grow." A straightforward, understandable application of cause and effect. I believe that this equation does apply to sales as well, but for my dad, his work and the compensation he received for it existed in a kind of parallel universe, one that had its own inexplicable rules, formed not through logic and predictability, but by emotion and happenstance. His efforts, in other words, often received no tangible reward. Since this applied to him, he would make it apply as well to creditors. If they requested payment in what he perceived to be an inappropriate way, well then, they would not be paid. As he was fond of saying, "The hell with them!" What he did then, and this is very important, he stopped thinking about them.

My mother, bless *her* heart, operated in the real world. She was the keeper of the checkbook. She was the one who discovered, when the bank called, that my dad had written checks for which funds were not available. Hers was the hard reality that when money wasn't there, consequences ensued, painful ones that my dad simply didn't want to face.

In terms of the financial factors that apply to your area of responsibility, you can't stop thinking about them! Don't assume that financial matters exist and operate in a parallel universe—that proverbial galaxy far, far away, the province of the controllers and the bean counters (they comprise, in fact, a "bean" that you need to keep moving). Whether you're completely aware of this or not, financial issues are inputs that you need to process *continually* in your capacity as a manager.

I want to just beat you over the head with this. I feel the need to because some managers, like my dad, appear to have a death wish in this regard. They ignore bedrock financial "rules" and handle their financial assets and obligations as if there's no tomorrow. Perhaps out of fear (which may have been my dad's problem) of what they'll discover, they simply refuse to pay the required attention. <u>Don't do this.</u> Acknowledge, confront and act on the financial variables that apply to your operation in a clear-eyed, knowledgeable, responsible and courageous manner.

When you do otherwise, you stick your head in the sand, and eventually that will suffocate you. Don't let it. The concepts covered in the rest of this chapter aren't rocket science. You can learn them. Your career could depend on how well you learn them (upper management loves people who understand "big picture" financial concepts); the success of your organization could well depend on how well you learn them.

<u>Application</u>

For my dad, money was a personal, emotional issue. As long as it remained that, his ability to control money rather than be controlled by it was limited. Like my dad, some managers and business owners simply say, "I don't want to think about it" when it comes to money management. As I suggested in an earlier chapter, they want to deal with the content of the business (the drywall and the plumbing), not the financial part.

Whether you are a department manager, a pastor, a CEO, or a small business owner, I recommend that you see yourself as a steward of the assets under your control, including of course the financial ones. Being a steward means that while you may not own these assets, you're responsible for them. It means assuming responsibility for the kind of paper purchased for use in your office, and for the ways it's used (it's not supposed to be wasted). It means assuming responsibility for hours worked as direct labor in your department; those are supposed to be at or below the budget projection for them under Cost of Goods Sold.

A Glossary of Key Terms

What follows is a brief glossary of financial terms.

Cash: Financial planners are fond of saying "Cash is king." What they mean by this is knowing where hard dollars are coming from, when they're coming, and knowing how long you get to keep them before using them to meet obligations. They're also fond of saying that you can be a profitable enterprise (i.e., it's costing you less to produce goods than what you're receiving in payment for them), but unless you manage cash *flow* successfully, you can find yourself out of business. They say that cash is the life blood of an enterprise, and they're right. To make a gruesome analogy, when an animal is hurt and "bleeds out," it dies; should enough cash "bleed out" of an organization without replenishment, the organization dies.

In large organizations cash management is in large part the province and the responsibility of the controller. In small businesses, the responsibility rests with the manager and his/her accountant. In your organization, the manager you report to may share key financial information with you (if he/she doesn't, you should ask for it), and when this occurs you need to make every effort to understand the factors in your organization (department) that affect cash flow, and do what you can to ensure that the flow remains positive.

We'll say more about this in a later section on financial projections. If you're the owner of a business, you can't be myopic in ensuring adequate cash flow (e.g., looking at sales exclusively to fund operations). If your business is seasonal or you simply hit slow patches, you need to look for alternative sources of capital, either borrowing it or seeking investment. The point is to identify these sources in advance, perhaps securing a line of credit, before the need for additional cash materializes.

Sales. Until there is a sale, there is no business (I always startle myself when I express this unyielding fact). The sales factor has a number of dimensions. The first is, you need to have a viable product or service. You need to be offering something that people are willing to pay for. You may be, for example, an excellent push mower repair person, and think that you can provide for your family by opening Stan's Push Mower Repair. Maybe you can. Before leasing (or buying) a building for your business, however, you need to ask yourself the "V Question," about viability. This question asks simply, "Is there a need for this product or service?" To answer, you need to ask related questions: How many customers can you reasonably expect? How much will you charge them? How long will basic repairs take? Will dollars come in equally throughout the year? What will you do if they don't?

Other dimensions are actual sales transactions—and who will engage in those transactions, yourself or a dedicated sales person?—and marketing. The latter refers to customers who must be contacted before sales can occur. You'll need to decide which customers (market segments) you'll approach, and in what manner. Again, the unyielding fact is no sales = no cash = no funds to pay salaries, overhead and operating expenses.

It's said that business is about acquiring and keeping customers. It's also said that it's easier to achieve sales to existing customers vs. finding new ones. In this core function everyone can play a part, either directly through contacting potential customers, working in marketing, or simply ensuring that extraordinary products and services are delivered to existing customers.

Cost of Goods Sold. Businesses need to produce or acquire goods and services for less than they receive in payment for them. The difference between these two amounts is called gross profit. In a clothing store, if you buy a suit for $100 and sell it for $150, gross profit is $50. We want to keep gross profit as high as possible; because out of gross profit we need to pay operating expenses (the rent and utilities), other expenses such as those for taxes and interest, and have something left over to plow back into the business as investment (you need to upgrade your window displays, to present your suits in the most favorable manner possible).

A factor that can keep gross profit low is competition. Pricing our goods and services is always a matter of covering our own cost for them, at the same time offering comparable or more favorable prices than those offered by our competitors. While we'd like to achieve the gross profit margins recommended for our specific kind of business, we may need to accept less—sometimes far less—in order to get the sale.

Direct labor factors heavily into cost of goods sold. You need to find and pay people who can "deliver the goods" for you, and this is often a tall order. Doing so is a large part of managing this part of your operation. On the one hand you need expert, reliable people, and on the other hand those people are hard to find and expensive to hire and retain. Finding the correct balance in this area is an ongoing challenge. We do get better at it that through time and experience.

Your other key responsibility in this area is minimizing waste, scrap and rework. All of these drive up the cost of both labor and materials. Training is often key to this. Make sure that people understand product specifications (quality), and how to perform the tasks and operate the equipment needed to create the product. A principle in this area is that it's best to build quality in through process improvement versus inspecting for defects after they've already happened. Once the defects have occurred, whether you discover them before the customer does or not—the cattle have already left the corral.

And you need to make sure that your people stay engaged in productive work. I've seen people relaxing on production lines reading newspapers, and my thought is always "We're buying this person's time, and we need to make sure we're getting our money's worth."

My examples above reflect manufacturing or process industries, but the principles apply to every organization. There is scrap and rework in accounting firms. There are bad, inefficient processes in every business; there are people in every organization who aren't producing as much as they might.

Operating Expenses. Mentioned above, these are your expenses for rent, utilities, office supplies, postage/delivery, and perhaps administrative personnel. Operating expenses are all those dollars you need to spend to keep your doors open, regardless of how much revenue may be coming in. They're also called fixed costs.

You probably can't save your way to prosperity (you need to grow your way), but everyone shares responsibility for preserving the organization's assets. Be alert for savings, even the smallest ones, as these will add up significantly over time. Pay attention to utility costs, seeing, for example, if you may be able to bundle services vs. paying for each separately. Do you really need daily janitorial services? If you do, do you need *all* the janitorial services you're contracting for now? Are you paying bills online, or still using envelopes and stamps? This is my penny in the parking lot principle. If I find a penny there today, that's one less that I need to earn tomorrow.

Interest, Taxes, Depreciation and Amortization. The IRS allows us to deduct expenses in these areas from income (also called earnings). This equation is referred to as EBITDA: Earnings Before Interest, Taxes, Depreciation and Amortization. You need to be aware of them because they do cost you money, just not as directly as the money you spend on the rent and the light bill. It's costing you to borrow money (interest), for example; you are obliged to pay income tax, and perhaps property and other taxes; and you remember that your tangible and intangible assets are eroding over time as depreciation and amortization.

Your tax advisor and attorney will be of more help in this area than I will be. I don't know, for example, the tax issues that affect your operation, and if one way of arranging those is more advantageous than another (e.g., whether it may be better for you to remain an LLC or become an S Corporation, or if it might be more advantageous to speed up depreciation on a building or piece of equipment vs. letting the depreciation run full term). I can advise you about debt and interest. As to the first, go into as little of it as possible; as to the second, find the lowest rates you can. If you need capital, don't be afraid to pursue so-called "alternative sources," individuals or groups who are looking to invest—perhaps in a company such as yours. You know what they say about banks; they'll lend you money only if you can prove you don't need it.

Equity. In what can be the hard scrabble effort to make a business successful, the concept of equity can receive less attention than it deserves. Equity is what a company is worth, expressed as a dollar amount. I say that it sometimes receives less attention than it deserves, because it's often difficult to think about the value of the enterprise when the future of the enterprise may be in immediate doubt. Difficult, that is, to think about the value of the *Titanic* when you're searching frantically for a lifeboat. This fact does not make the concept of equity any less important.

Equity is determined by subtracting a company's liabilities (what it owes) from its assets (what it owns). Equity shows up on balance sheets, financial reports that always balance out the two variables. This is shown as assets always equaling liabilities plus equity. If total assets equal $1,000, and total liabilities equal $750, then equity is $250. The balancing part is $750 + $250 = $1,000.

Lenders love "healthy balance sheets" (substantial equity) because they generally indicate that a company is doing what it needs to in order to fund current and future operations. This is not always the case. Assets include investments, and perhaps a benefactor is misguidedly pouring dollars into a company without proper due diligence—the study required to ensure that the operation is sound and the future promising. Equity can be low or even negative, especially at startup when companies are acquiring the assets needed for operation, but it shouldn't remain so for appreciable periods of time. My guidance about equity is simply watch it; watch it from year to year. If it isn't increasing, at least understand why it isn't, and, if appropriate, make plans to reverse that direction.

Net Profit. Net profit is shown on a financial document called an income statement. Income statements are snapshots of where a company is at a moment in time, showing sales, cost of goods, gross profit, operating expenses, EBITDA, ITDA (interest, taxes, depreciation and amortization costs), and finally sales minus all of the foregoing equals net profit.

Sales

-Cost of Goods =

Gross Profit

-Operating Expenses =

EBITDA

-Interest, Taxes, Depreciation and Amortization =

Net Profit

Retained Earnings. Businesses report their income on a yearly basis. At the end of calendar or fiscal years, usually their accountants "do the numbers" and report to owners or shareholders what the company accomplished financially over the course of the year—in all of the categories just described. Diminishing liabilities? That's good. Sales higher than projections? That's good. Fixed costs eroding profits? Not so good. Year-end financials also report a number called "retained earnings," and this reflects dollars invested back into the company. It's left over, so to speak, instead of being drawn out for different reasons (such as a trip to Bermuda). Auditors and potential investors like to see substantial retained earnings, as they indicate that management is not required to—or chooses not to—squeeze every single dollar earned out of the operation.

Dollars left in the company comprise internal capital available to fund ongoing operations or perhaps upgrade those operations. The alternative is to seek those funds through borrowing or perhaps taking on partners, which means additional interest expense if you choose the first option, and reduced control and profit for you if you choose the second.

<u>Financial Projections</u>

We will talk more about business planning in a later chapter, but you need to understand one more crucial financial factor pertaining to them. Every business needs to *project* how it hopes to perform over a period covering at least three years. This means, for example, after diligent examination of past performance (if this is possible), estimating the sales dollars you expect to come in. You often divide sales projections into categories. Our clothing store owner will divide projected sales into those expected for suits, outerwear, shirts, and accessories.

In a similar way, you break out your anticipated cost of goods—what the suits, outerwear, shirts and accessories will cost, including the cost of the labor needed to sell them. The same then occurs for operating expenses: you project that you'll spend $10 in January for postage and delivery, $500 for utilities (it's going to be cold), the inexorable $1,500 for rent, and so on.

You can create these kinds of projections using Excel spreadsheets or dedicated business planning software. Whatever application or method you use should report numbers as Projected, Actual and Variance. That simply means what you hope the numbers will be (okay, "estimate" is a better word than "hope"); what they actually are; and the difference between those two variables. The latter is important, because with the variance number you can express percentages—saying to yourself, for example, "Wow! What we paid for daffodils turned out to be 25% more than we'd estimated!" The higher the variance amounts, the greater the need to return to the drawing board and examine that item more carefully.

All of the above assumes that you have a budget (projection) for your operation. If there is one and you don't know what it is or where it is, you're flying blind. Ask for one, then clasp it to your bosom with the proverbial hoops of steel. When your manager appears at your door to ask how you're doing, you need to reach into your top drawer, smile, ask about her family, retrieve the budget, and say, "In terms of which category? We've made real savings this month in terms of rework, which is running 8% lower than last month, but there are other 'pluses' I want to talk about as well." Then talk about them.

Managing to the Numbers

The situation just described is a significant departure from our manager discussed in Chapter One. This was the unfortunate individual, who, when asked what she was doing, responded, "Same old, same old." It's within the realm of financial management that you, by contrast, can shine.

If we're not "managing to the numbers," what in the name of all that's sacred are we doing? Of course, you'll say, "We're managing our people!" And God, and perhaps upper management, will say "Bless you for doing that." In fact, people management is a key part of financial management (as we saw, bottom lines diminish if people aren't productive enough; if they are absentee or discipline problems; or if they sue the company).

But besides and/or in addition to people management, creating projections and monitoring actual numbers against those projections is a vital way that you keep score in your business or organization. If you don't know how, you put yourself at an enormous disadvantage. While this kind of ignorance—or refusal to confront reality—can be blissful for a while, it is not sustainable.

In short, financial management is a vital dimension of how you see and carry out your responsibilities. If your head has been in the sand in terms of this dimension, don't let it go there again. Stand up straight, get the sand out of your eyes, and say to yourself, "I can do this; the organization needs me to do this." It does, and you can.

For Further Consideration

1. Has talking about money been off limits to any degree, either in your personal or business life? Why in your specific case has this been true?

2. How does the description of you as a financial manager strike you? Explain your answer. If you haven't perceived yourself this way, why haven't you?

3. Why do you think individuals in both their private and business lives sometimes refuse to acknowledge the fact that financial matters are important and deserve attention? What is it about money matters, in other words, that appears to be so threatening? Can you think of ways that this fear can be alleviated? What are they?

4. How does cash flow affect you, both personally and in your working life? If you see improvement in the area of cash management as being important, can you think of ways to do so more successfully? Whom or what could you enlist to help you in your efforts? What has kept you from enlisting such assistance in the past?

5. Many who contemplate going into business for themselves identify sales and marketing as problematic areas—areas they're least comfortable working in. Given the importance of this function (there is no business until there's a sale), how can we approach it with more confidence, and how can we acquire needed skill?

6. When you think about cost of goods in your operation, which do you see as the most significant (i.e., those

reflecting the greatest dollar amounts)? If it were up to you, can you identify ways that costs in these areas could be reduced? What are some specific suggestions you have?

7. Explain the concept of equity as it's presented on an organization's balance sheet.

8. In your current position, do you "manage to the numbers"? If not, do you think it possible to develop the projections you'd need in order to do so? Whom could you enlist to help you in this effort?

10 PLANNING

<u>Has Its Day Passed?</u>

To be honest with you, Mark Zuckerberg is starting to get on my nerves. One of his practices at Facebook is what he calls "Hackathons" (I read about this in the train magazine recently on my way home from Philadelphia). Hackathons are all-night sessions in which Facebook people compete with one another to come up with new ideas. They don't get paid for this—they do it because they enjoy it. As author Gregory Ferenstein puts it, "They enjoy working an all-night shift because it's essentially one big party celebrating their geekdom." [1]

What's up with that? I'm trying to write this sensible, meat and potatoes book here, and Zuckerberg is promoting these chaotic parties? And they're *working*? Our subtitle of this book is *A Framework for Guiding Success in the Workplace*. I like words like "framework" and "guiding." I like structure. I just don't know about these parties!

But the more I think about it, the less steamed I become at Mark. He is, in fact, doing things that I've touched on previously, and the hackathons are an example of what I'm about to talk about in this chapter. In terms of the former, Zuckerberg realizes how important his people are; he needs all the creative energy he can get from them. Second, he realizes that he needs to engage in "out of the box" activities to tap that potential, and the hackathons are an example of his willingness to do that. And finally (and this addresses our current purpose), the hackathons don't occur randomly or haphazardly. They exist as part of a plan. I guess the parties themselves are frameworks, and through them, Mark is guiding people in a definite direction.

In this chapter we're going to talk about planning: looking at different aspects or dimensions of your job, how you manage people, money, compliance and so on. This chapter not only represents a dimension that you need to manage, but it infuses the way you manage all the others. Do I need to say that again? Okay: it's a key topic and area in its own right that all managers need to be aware of and hopefully excel in. It also, if you let it, informs (suffuses) the way you approach all the rest of your responsibilities.

<u>We Don't Like to Plan</u>

I like this quotation:

> *Planning is an unnatural process; it is much more fun to do something. The nicest thing about not planning is that failure comes as a complete surprise, rather than being preceded by a period of worry and depression.* [2]   *Sir John Harvey-Jones*

The part I want to spend a moment on is "it is much more fun to do something." This is what I see, especially in small businesses. It *is* more fun to do something. As mentioned earlier, entrepreneurs start businesses because they like and are good at the *content* of the business: tax preparation, house painting, landscaping, printing, construction, plumbing. We're drawn to those things we're good at, and it's natural that we want to engage in those things vs. unfamiliar tasks involving business planning, human resources and accounting. First line manufacturing supervisors would much rather be up to their elbows in their operations (even turning wrenches in some cases), rather than in their offices developing staffing projections.

What we're talking about in part is "the appeal of the urgent," the "catching" that we talked about earlier. We love surprises! We are excited about the prospect of what could happen next! Who knows who might walk through the door next, with an order for ten million landscape pavers?! Related to this, we might love being the "answer man" in the company—the go-to man or woman who understands every nano-detail of the business. We can't plan! We have to be ready for the next emergency! Each emergency provides us with a "rush" in and of itself, and it also "primes" us for the next one. Each is a rehearsal for the next act in the drama.

There is so much wrong with this picture. Perhaps the most important is that key areas of management responsibility can remain undone—in the excitement of putting out the latest fire. Compliance? The incorrect I-9 Forms lying in a desk somewhere? The Hazard Communication, "Right to Know" program that you are required, REQUIRED to have? The supervisors selecting internal candidates for open positions because they are a good "fit"? Hispanic employees asking if the employee handbook can be made available in Spanish? The two forklift drivers who haven't had certification training?

These and other key areas of responsibility can be left unattended. They remain so until they spontaneously combust (as in an employee lawsuit or an accident), and then they too can be handled as the crisis of the moment.

It's a model that is unsustainable. People will burn out. Critical, perhaps fatal mistakes will be made (those uncertified forklift drivers may run into someone). The operation will be wasteful and inefficient. People will become discouraged and disillusioned, and eventually leave. Relationships among departments will deteriorate. Little new, creative, productive thinking will occur.

Okay, okay; perhaps I overstate my case just a *tad*, but you need to allow me my key points: with Sir Harvey-Jones we can agree that planning is something of an unnatural activity (it's what ants do naturally, and what grasshoppers have trouble with); and second, there can be dire consequences if we don't engage in it, if we don't become proactive instead of reactive in processing the inputs coming at us. We need to plan how we're going to manage those little guys.

Planning in Context

This is a complicated, serious issue. How do you train yourself to plan systematically in a rapidly changing environment?

Does the latter actually preclude the former? How do you sit down, organizer (electronic or hardcopy) in hand, to plan the execution of your responsibilities, when the very floor under your feet seems to be fluid? When it feels like you're up to your neck in those alligators?

An example that's often given to illustrate the need for planning is vacations. We plan those vacations. We map out how far we'll get the first day, where we'll stay; we budget for gas, meals and hotels. Those of us who do business planning ask potential customers, "Don't you think your *business* deserves the same kind of detailed planning that you apply to your vacations?" It's a tough sell.

And perhaps the biggest reason for that tough sell is the maelstrom of activity that managers deal with on a daily basis. Until we acknowledge that, and the difficulty of planning within it, business owners and managers will look at us as if we're speaking Swahili.

<u>Making Serious Plans</u>

Maelstrom or no, I think we need to apply the vacation planning paradigm to our working lives as managers. We have to make plans. We have to have purpose and intention when we arrive at work. What are the priorities of the day? Which will we tackle first? How are going to tackle them? What kind of resources do we need to be successful? What are the factors most likely to derail us? How will we address those?

Any endeavor of any size or complexity needs to be planned. From a trip to the grocery store to the Allied invasion of

Normandy in 1944—if we don't map out what we hope to accomplish, listing in the process what might go wrong and what we'll do if it does—the likelihood of our accomplishing it is dramatically diminished.

Have you ever done project planning? Project management is a discipline all its own, but many of its tenets and principles apply to the kind of day-to-day business/organization planning we're talking about. You've seen Gantt Charts and PERT Charts, right?

Gantt Charts are the brainchild of one Henry Gantt. Basically, these charts and their accompanying methodology provide us with a project schedule, one showing all important tasks, when we might accomplish them, and, very importantly, the related tasks that must be completed before others can be begun and accomplished—that is, which tasks *depend* on one another for successful project completion.

Gantt charts have a cousin, the so-called PERT (Program Evaluation Review Technique) Chart, which was developed in the 1950's, and was vital to the military's development of the Polaris Submarine Program.

These planning tools are part of the Critical Path Method (CPM), which began as the "civilian" variation of PERT—the application of the Polaris Submarine planning methodology to business and organizational planning. At the heart of these methods is that to accomplish a "serious" project, you need to be clear about what it is you want to do; you need to think about "dependent" factors that must be addressed and sequenced along the way in order to complete your main objective; and you need to think of contingent actions to take should interruptions and obstacles get in the way of your originally planned activities.

Do I want you to bring this kind of systematic planning rigor to your day-to-day life as a manager?

Actually, I do.

This kind of planning is sometimes associated with an overall kind of management which those of us in the discipline speak of only in the most hushed of tones: it's. . ."micro-management." Micro-management for the most part has negative connotations; it occurs when managers have their fingers too deeply into every pie in their respective areas of responsibility. In so doing they slow progress and tend to squelch the contributions of others.

But so-called micro-management is more about execution or administration than it is about content. It's the *way* you might choose to go about any of your managerial tasks, planning included. My feeling is that you can use all the planning tools described above and not micro-manage; all the tools are doing is laying out what it is that must be accomplished—they don't dictate a specific way that project activities must occur.

I understand that your duties as a manager may not comprise a "project" per se. Those duties, however, might be better accomplished if we envisioned them that way: as discrete "agenda items" that will take some time, attention and effort to address.

Each duty or responsibility, remember, is one of those beans that we need to keep moving. I'm simply saying that each is best not left to chance. If I were your manager, I would want you to tell me in detail how you plan to keep each one moving across the field. If you want to put a Gantt or PERT Chart in front of me to help you explain—knock yourself out.

Filters Revisited

This of course is what I talked about earlier, about the need to filter things, about the need to prioritize. I could add to the image that I created in Chapter Five, when I talked about sliding the daily filter into the "pipeline" bringing inputs to you. I could add a valve upstream of where you are, which you could use to limit the entry of potential inputs in the first place. This is what you do when you plan your minutes, hours and days.

If such an "upstream" mechanism were available, you would not only be able to control the inputs already in the pipeline; you could shut them off at the source. In old movies we see a boss saying to his secretary, "Marie, hold my calls!" That boss is closing valves that could have allowed other, less important inputs into the mix.

This concept is key to the question I pose in this section: how do you retain your priorities, and perhaps your sanity, in the environment you now occupy? A big part of the answer is planning. At its heart planning is first identifying important things, prioritizing them, then devising strategies to address them in sustainable ways. If not the Gantt and PERT Charts, it's at least some kind of formal identification of your main areas of responsibility and how you propose to address them. It's what you write into that Position Agreement Form.

Laying things out this way provides a *framework* for the decision making you do moment-to-moment. It's bringing order to what can rapidly become disorder.

Let's return now to something a bit more earthy—this "pond" that we envisioned your jumping into each day on the job. Here's what may be an obvious point: you can't jump into the water *first* and then figure out how you're going to deal with the alligators! You need to say to yourself at least the day before, "Tomorrow I'm going to be in that pond, and I know the alligators will be there too. What will I do before I jump in? After I jump in? What if a given alligator is bigger than I thought he'd be?" And very importantly, "*Is anyone going to be jumping in with me?*"

At some point you need to do the filtering exercise we discussed earlier. You label each alligator in some form of plan. You find a screen and make an alligator-specific label for it (such as "Develop Hazcom Plan"). In this way, both long term and short term, daily and monthly, you anticipate what may come at you, and do the best you can to prepare for it.

First Things First

Remember the First Law of Filters: not everything gets through. As you saw in our figure in Chapter Five, you do have to leave that screen in place for Screaming Crises. But note again the size of that screen in proportion to the others. Sizing the screen in that way is a *decision* that you make, one based on the Position Agreement Form and the importance and urgency of the items you included on it.

Do you know how Stonewall Jackson got his nickname in the Civil War? During the first battle of Bull Run, while Confederate lines were in danger of breaking, Jackson and his brigade stood firm. Another Confederate Officer, Brigadier General Barnard Elliott Bee, Jr., allegedly cried out, "There is Jackson standing like a stone wall. Let us determine to die here, and we will conquer. Rally behind the Virginians!" [3]

Of the many options before him, Jackson acted on the one to which he'd assigned the highest priority: at that moment, with the outcome of that battle perhaps on the line, he chose both for himself personally and for the men under his command to stand firm—like a stone wall.

A manager's "stance" in the face of what comes at him/her on a daily basis is different in degree, but not in kind. Decisions about what to do, what to pick up and what to let lie, have to be made on the basis of what's important. As I just said, this needs to be decided in advance, and it can't be just the playing out of a preconceived battle plan. I would argue that it has to *start* with that battle plan, but after that is conceived and put into action, what happens moment-to-moment is dictated by both adherence to the plan and by the exigencies that develop. "Exigencies" are those matters that require immediate attention.

Deciding which matter to pick up and which to let lie is not just a matter of making a plan and then executing it (allowing for the aforementioned exigencies). It is in many cases a matter of character and principle as well. You designed your filters according to your best idea of what's expected of you on your job. You documented that work in a Position Agreement.

The planning endeavor as a whole allows you to respond systematically to all dimensions of your job (even diverting some as you need to), but rarely can you deal effectively with more than one or two at a time. To stick with your Agreement, dealing with the inputs that you deem most important moment-to-moment, takes the just-mentioned character, and it also takes courage. Not everyone "stands like a stone wall," but this is not a bad image, and practice, for us to embrace.

Paradigms Revisited

I would argue that Mark Zuckerberg acts according to plan; I would say that Stonewall Jackson did as well. To me people need a "vision," a perception, a paradigm if you will, of how they're going to approach their jobs as managers. They have to look through a prism at the variety and complexity that face them daily. Rather than shapelessness stretching as far as the eye can see (interrupted by crises as they develop), they need a structure, one supplied by a plan.

I'm reminded that the nature of a lens determines in large part what is seen. Any collective activity (e.g. Civil War battle or football game) is best "seen" through the lens of a plan, one undergirded by strong character and sound principles. There will always be those more-than-pesky exigencies, but they're best handled within the framework of a plan. You can swat a fly much more easily in a room than you can outside.

Is that just hopelessly obvious? Do cooks proceed without recipes? Pilots without flight plans? Actors without scripts? Builders without blueprints? Teachers without lesson plans? Generals without battle plans?

Managers, pastors, and business owners need plans. Further, I would argue that they need foundations of character and principle to support those plans. Taken together, the plan and the foundation become bulwarks in the face of the daily maelstrom. You can't be blown away by the crisis of the moment if you have this structure and this foundation.

Hmmmm. I think I have been co-opted in presenting this point by one of those three little pigs! Drat! The one that built the house out of bricks! Lots of huffing and puffing occurred, as I recall, but the plan worked. Neither the house nor the pig got blown away.

But—A Business Plan?

I need to close this chapter by talking at least briefly about the importance of formal business plans. Regardless of their different positions and areas of responsibility, I think all managers need to understand them—and have them! Put most simply, business plans spell out who and what you are, what you hope to accomplish, and how you plan to accomplish it.

They differentiate you from your competitors, paying attention to both strengths and weaknesses (both yours and those of your competitors). They recognize that you can't be all things to all potential markets, so they help you identify the most promising markets and the strategies you'll need to approach and sell to them successfully. Very importantly (we made this point earlier), they give you targets to shoot for in the form of financial projections (those for sales, cost of goods, expenses and other important targets). Staffing plans within business plans help you determine how many and what kind of people you'll need to reach your goals.

The financial issues and concepts discussed in the last chapter play a prominent role in business planning (remember they are an important way that we keep score), but other matters also receive attention. Among these are an organization's vision, mission and values. Clarifying these matters strengthens the framework I described above. Recall how this played out in the Tylenol situation discussed earlier. What did Johnson & Johnson decide to do to process that particular input (the presence of deadly contaminants in their product)? They processed it in light of a commitment they'd made to the good health of their customers. This commitment, (reflective of their vision and values) was articulated as part of the business planning process.

In short, your business plan should be among the most primary of ways that you deal with the day-to-day conduct of your department, business or organization. It is in essence the basis of the framework that we talked about; until it is hoisted into place, you have nothing upon which to hang the rest of the structure. It articulates the priorities that guide your moment-to-moment, day-to-day reactions to the issues that confront you.

The literature in this area is full of step-by-step guidance in the preparation of business plans. I recommend strongly that you access that information and act on it. Remember the paradigm: look at your responsibilities through the sturdy framework supplied by a plan, a framework within which predictable, sustainable results appear, grow and multiply.

For Further Consideration

1. Would people characterize you as "an organized person"? Why or why not? How do you rate organizational skill as a factor in overall personal or professional success? Explain your answer.
2. Do you agree with the point made in this chapter that people don't like to plan? What are your own explanations for why this might be the case?
3. Why is planning a vacation simpler somehow than planning a day's or week's activity in the workplace? How can you make planning in the workplace as productive as the planning you would do for a vacation?
4. In your own working situation, what urgent consider-ations affect you on a consistent basis? Remember that urgent matters (exigencies) are those that require immediate attention. Can you differentiate important

from less important exigencies? If so, are there ways you can keep the less important ones from occupying your time and attention? How might you do this?

5. Could you employ a "Marie, hold my calls!" tactic in your operation? If not, what variations on that practice might work? If not Marie, in other words, who might hold your calls?

6. The recommendation in this chapter is that you make plans before "jumping into the pond" that might contain alligators. Is this doable for you? What might your process be for putting such a plan together? When, for example, would you do it?

7. What do you think of the idea of micro-management? Do you agree that using some of the project management tools discussed in this chapter could characterize a person this way? Do you think that's a bad thing? Are there areas of your responsibility that would lend themselves well to this particular approach?

8. Do you get the idea of a sturdy planning framework—that such a framework is necessary for the successful execution of your responsibilities? That within such a framework you can allow for the kind of creative activities engaged in by the Mark Zuckerbergs of the world? Planning can be the actual frame of reference or paradigm through which you perceive your duties and responsibilities. Describe this framework as it currently exists for you. If you perceive it as less than effective, what changes can you identify that would make it more so? Whom could you enlist to help you?

Notes

1. Ferenstein, Gregory. "Earnest Money." *Arrive* September/October 2011: 42-44. Print.
2. "Sir John Harvey-Jones." *Man in a Shed*. Web. 10 Jan. 2008.
3. "Thomas 'Stonewall' Jackson 1824-1863." City-On-A-Hill. Web. 17 Nov. 2011.

11 EQUAL IN THE EYES OF THE LAW

<u>Compliance</u>

A main theme in this book is that you have to see your job as a manager whole. You can't focus solely on production or perhaps the technical or creative aspects of the job that appeal to you. A hard fact is that the workplace is a legal jungle, and if you aren't aware of that generally, and of specific legal/regulatory requirements specifically, you can get both yourself and your organization into a great deal of trouble.

Do you recall in the last chapter, I mentioned that before jumping into an alligator-filled pond you should see if anyone is jumping in with you? In terms of compliance, you'll want to ask your HR people to jump in with you. If there are more alligators than even they can handle, they'll recruit legal counsel to help as well. But a big part of compliance responsibility will always reside with you. You, as it were, are the first line of defense, and you need to be aware, vigilant and prepared.

What I want to concentrate on in this and the following two compliance-related chapters are the specific areas that you touch as a manager that have serious compliance impli-cations. If you know they're there, even though you may not become an expert, you'll at least have some broad guidance as to what kinds of actions and behaviors on your part are compliant, and which potentially are not.

Here is my primary piece of advice: if you have even the slightest inkling that something you're contemplating (perhaps a disciplinary action) may not be entirely compliant, ask someone for help. This could be your HR representative, legal counsel or your immediate supervisor. When these people are not immediately available, you could do an online search of the issue and acquire information that way. Don't rely on your own perceptions and inclinations, because those can be peculiarly your own! When in doubt about a particular course of action, ask.

Or, as I'm about to suggest, read the appropriate *policy*!

The Role of Policies

Perhaps your organization has formal policies and work rules. It would be an even more blessed state of affairs if those have been modified and updated frequently, keeping pace with new laws and regulations as those have emerged. If your organization has these resources, they are your first line of defense in terms of doing the right thing. The policies, you see, reflect laws with which we in the workplace need to comply.

It is not strictly a policy matter, but other virtually indispensable documents you should have in your organization are job descriptions. Job descriptions help immensely in warding off potential legal trouble, especially as they delineate clearly "essential job functions," those that people aspiring to specific jobs must be able to perform. They delineate as well conditions under which these essential functions are carried out, and in this way communicate what people must be ready for in undertaking a given job.

To return to policies per se, if you have a policy that guarantees everyone equal employment opportunity regardless of any protected category (e.g. age, race, national origin, disabling condition), then all you worry about is adhering to the policy. If you have a privacy policy, you follow that policy, and that will preclude your shaking down employees at your whim, on the suspicion that they may be concealing drugs or stealing company secrets (or socket wrenches). You let the policy do the heavy lifting.

I wish I could end this chapter with that last section on policies, and trust that that simple action would address all your current and future compliance issues. It won't. Even in organizations with robust policies and strong policy administration practices (for keeping policies current and available), two things can occur. First, situations will arise that may fall into a gray policy area—where no definitive right or wrong answer suggests itself. When this occurs you (and your

155

HR people) rely on precedent, similar issues that surfaced in the past, to guide you, in addition to the guidance you find in your policies. Sometimes nothing will do but simply talking through the issue with stakeholders affected by it until you arrive at a reasonable course of action.

Second, a manager, often without the proper forethought, will take matters into his or her own hands and do the inappropriate thing. We managers are human beings, and human beings can act out of ignorance (with the best of intentions) and we can also simply make errors in judgment. When this occurs, job descriptions, policies and work rules in and of themselves are often not sufficient. Broader knowledge of the legal framework *surrounding* your policies should produce better decisions, sounder judgments.

If you don't have job descriptions, policies and an employee handbook that reflects the policies, I strongly advise that you acquire and distribute them as soon as you can. With this general recommendation, let's look now at several broad areas that you should be mindful of in terms of compliance.

<u>Equal Employment Opportunity</u>

The Civil Rights Act of 1964 made it illegal to discriminate against people on the basis of race, color, religion, sex, or national origin. Later legislation expanded protections to those in other categories, such as people with disabilities and those over forty years of age. Title VII of the Act is the part of the law that deals with protection of individuals in these categories in matters of their employment. The message for you is, don't discriminate against individuals in the workplace because of their race, color, religion, sex, national origin, age or disability. "Discriminate against" refers to treating people in these categories differently—which means don't treat them worse than you do others, barring them from opportunities that they have a legal right to. Don't treat them better either, as doing that can invite claims of reverse discrimination.

The intent of the Civil Rights Act (CRA) wasn't to establish quotas, saying that employers needed to hire and promote specific percentages of individuals in the various protected categories. Rather, it was designed to level the playing field for people in those categories; it was to give them access to opportunities that they'd been denied.

As a manager, you touch virtually all the "terms, conditions and privileges" of your employees' working lives. In all likelihood you have a say in their initial employment, often doing at least some interviewing of candidates. After they're hired, you evaluate your employees' performance; ensure that their compensation is equitable and administered properly (you don't actually perform the latter function, but you may intercede when it is incorrect); ensure that their performance and behavior are acceptable; promote or demote them as their performance allows/demands; and you may be the person who recommends that a given employee leave the organization.

In all these and other employment actions, you are enjoined by Title VII of the CRA to proceed not on the basis of any protected category (e.g. age, gender or national origin), but solely on the basis of how well the individual is carrying out the specific duties and responsibilities of his or her job, or, in the case of someone applying for a job, how that individual's qualifications match the knowledge and skills you're looking for. Job related qualifications, in other words, are everything. Attitudes and feelings are much less than everything. "Gut feelings" in particular are to be avoided in making employment decisions.

Let me mention, in light of the above, the idea that an individual to you may not look like a "good fit" for a certain position. I don't like the idea of good fits. Sometimes, as a matter of fact, a *bad* fit may be just what is needed in a given instance. A business or department isn't a club; it's a group of people qualified to carry out a set of specialized activities. We don't need homogeneity—which means we don't need everyone looking, talking and thinking exactly alike. Diversity can be of great value, in the way that it brings differing perspectives and talents to the table. So look for that: look for talent, qualifications, and the apparent will to put them to work enthusiastically in your organization—not for people who "fit" comfortably.

As you engage in your employee-related responsibilities, be careful of documents in which you record information about your employees—for example shorthand notes you may take during an interview. Watch where you keep these documents; don't, for example, put everything you record about an employee into his or her personnel file. The only thing that should be in a personnel file is information pertaining to that employee's performance (prior performance in the case of an application, current performance in the case of performance evaluations completed by an immediate supervisor). In the event of legal action, all information pertaining to a case is discoverable (attachable as evidence by the complainant's counsel), so the watchword is be careful what you keep.

Let's look briefly at a scenario with EEO implications. An individual comes to interview for a job, one that requires considerable physical dexterity—including the ability to go up and down steep ladders regularly. You notice that the candidate in front of you has only one leg. When asked if she is able to perform all the physical requirements of the job, she responds in the affirmative. What do you do? What you do is say to her, "Would you mind demonstrating for me how you'd climb the ladders in our warehouse?" And you would allow her that opportunity.

Here is why you don't draw attention to the candidate's apparent disability. You may be this wonderful, caring person. When you notice that your candidate is missing a leg, your tendency may be to ask about it, and, heaven forbid, express sympathy. Don't do that. In terms of EEO considerations, we never want to elicit information from candidates that we could use to discriminate against them. It doesn't matter what your intentions are. It doesn't matter that you have no intention of using the information in a discriminatory manner. In court, plaintiff's attorney will ask why you asked about her missing leg. You will say, "I was just curious and concerned, as any sensitive, thoughtful person would be."

Plaintiff's attorney will say, "That's all well and good, but it's really a pretext. You were asking because you knew she could become a 'problem child' in your department, perhaps requiring special attention of various kinds, and you just didn't want that kind of additional hassle." You don't want to put yourself in the position of having to respond to this kind of allegation.

A side note on this particular example: advances in prosthetic devices are occurring so rapidly that you probably wouldn't notice a missing appendage, nor would the individual using such a device be at a significant disadvantage in his or her ability to perform.

What you can do, as stated above, is ask the candidate to demonstrate how she would carry out one or more of the essential functions of the position. Here's another point: if you place that requirement on her (climbing the ladder), you must place it on every other candidate who applies for that job. All you care about, in short, is people's ability to perform those essential requirements. The missing leg? You don't see it; you don't mention it. We'll talk more about employees with disabilities in our next chapter.

Sexual Harassment

Sexual harassment is prohibited in the workplace. It is a subsection of discrimination on the basis of sex. As a manager, you are to avoid at all costs *quid pro quo* ("something for something") sexual harassment. In these instances, managers condition opportunities for advancement and/or threats of reprisal on an employee's willingness to exchange sexual favors. In other words, "The promotion is yours if you agree to sleep with me." Should a person be found culpable (guilty) of this form of harassment, he or she becomes personally liable, and in all likelihood loses any partial protection that could have been afforded him/her as an agent of the company.

The other form of sexual harassment is called hostile environment harassment. In this form, sexually-oriented "content" of all kinds is pervasive in the workplace, from objectionable pictures in tool boxes to inappropriate jokes and comments that are sexually oriented. The environment can become so permeated with these kinds of objects and activities that people can no longer work comfortably, and when this occurs, they bring hostile environment complaints. If management "knows or should have known" that the environment existed, personal and corporate liability increase. As a manager or supervisor, you need to take responsibility for the workplace that you supervise; this means all of its "content." If this content is objectionable, you need to take immediate steps to correct it.

Sexual harassment is not the only kind. Harassment on the basis of any protected category—national origin, age, race, pregnancy, disability—is illegal. Thus you don't make jokes about people's age, nor do you allow others to; you don't isolate people whose first language is not English; you don't allow prejudicial comments about those who come from minority cultures (e.g. Asian, South Asian or Hispanic cultures). Again, the one most likely to know about and act on harassment is you; it's a responsibility you need to take seriously.

Here is a general watchword about harassment, perhaps especially about sexual harassment. When we were first doing sexual harassment training, we watched an excellent video in which the narrator said, "If you find yourself tempted to say or do something you're afraid might be discriminatory or inappropriate, ask yourself, if your child or significant other were standing next to you, would you say it or do it? If not, don't say it, don't do it." Good advice. Don't say it, don't do it.

Affirmative Action

Another effort to ensure equal employment opportunity became law in 1965 when President Johnson issued Executive Order 11246, which required employers doing business with the Federal Government (having contracts valued at $50,000 or more, or smaller contracts matching or exceeding that value), to act "affirmatively" to prevent discrimination in their employment practices on the basis of the same qualities identified in Title VII. Acting affirmatively means doing something before someone *requires* that you do it.

Those covered by Executive Order 11246 don't need to hire or promote specific numbers of people in the categories identified. Rather, they do need to act "affirmatively," making reasonable efforts to make the numbers of people in those categories roughly equal to those available, both inside their organizations and in the immediately surrounding areas. Covered employers need to create Affirmative Action Plans

(AAPs), in which they report the numbers of women and minorities employed by Job Group (e.g. Executives, Managers, Technicians, and so on), versus those available to be hired into those groups. Should reports show significant disparities between those available and those employed, the AAP needs to identify actions the employer is taking to correct the imbalance. Plans submitted under EO 11246 must be submitted separately from two other kinds of affirmative action plans.

These include plans associated with Section 503 of the Rehabilitation Act of 1974, which report the employment status of individuals with disabilities, and those associated with the Viet Nam Era Veterans' Readjustment Act (VEVRAA) which does the same for veterans. These latter kinds of AAPs are often submitted together.

Once again, the laws and EOs protecting various categories of individuals have nothing to do with guarantees and quotas. They have everything to do with leveling a playing field which had previously been anything but level. It's a matter of guaranteeing *access* to opportunity. As a manager, you are to understand this principle and make it part of your everyday working mentality.

Employment at Will

Employment at will isn't a law or a regulation; it's a governing principle. It states that either party in the employment relationship can end the relationship at any time, with or without cause. In other words, if you tire of your current employment situation, you can leave it. By the same token (supposedly), your employer can say to you "Carlos, I just don't like the tie you're wearing today. You're fired."

Except, employers can't really fire you, Carlos, because they don't like your tie. You, manager or supervisor, can't do this either, as one who may have hiring and firing authority. What has happened over the years is that employers' ability to do this has been "eroded" by any number of common law court decisions. "Wrongful Discharge," in other words, isn't a law— it's come to describe any number of employee separations from their organizations in which the terminated individual claims that he/she has been injured or harmed by that action. These are so-called tort claims, and their common denominator is that someone has been harmed or injured by the action of another.

Increasingly courts are viewing employees' jobs as actual possessions, highly valued ones, and those possessions are to be taken only after the most careful consideration. When contemplating separating someone from your organization, seek guidance from HR and legal. Most HR departments have checklists to work through (these are also available online), to ensure that every "i" is dotted and every "t" is crossed before taking this final step with an employee.

Unions

Union contracts don't guarantee equal employment opportunity in the same way the civil rights laws do. Rather, they represent agreements negotiated between management and a union as to how union members are to be treated (that would be equally), under the Fair Labor Standards Act (FLSA) generally, and under the provisions of an individual union contract specifically.

Unions are still powerful in certain industries (the auto industry for example), but their influence on the whole has diminished over the past several decades, with less than 10% of employees in the private sector now represented by unions. In large part this is because laws have been enacted that address many of the issues for which unions came to exist—those having to do with equal pay for example, and those just discussed that deal with discrimination. If you're a manager in a union shop you know the issues that come with managing in that "milieu." If not, you face the possibility that your company could be targeted by a union, and you need to be prepared for that eventuality.

One reason that employees opt for union representation is perceived lack of fairness on the part of management. Should this perception be strong enough, they may seek union representation and with it its perceived advantages in attaining higher pay, better benefits, and greater control of their working lives. Whether these enhancements ever come to fruition following a union election is another matter; I'm simply stating the most usual argument in unions' favor.

In my experience unions create barriers between employees and employers, one result of which is lessened ability on the part of management to actually manage the organization. They can still do so, but they must remain ever mindful of

FLSA requirements and the specific stipulations outlined in the union contract.

So if you don't have unions in your organization now, you may want to engage in those employee relations activities most likely to head off a desire for union representation in the first place. I'm talking about such things as reward and recognition programs, the opportunity to work flexible schedules, job sharing, all-employee events such as picnics, generous benefits and other "perks," and so on. In a sense, management is continually "selling" the organization to its employees through its total reward programs and employee relations efforts.

A potentially larger determinant, however, is the day-to-day perception that employees have that their managers are going to be there for them, that they, so to speak, "have their backs." If they perceive managers as having their backs, they will be less likely to seek a union to take over that function.

In terms of compliance, should you become involved in a union organizing campaign, there are definite rules that you will have to follow, the description of which is outside the scope of this chapter. Should you engage in unfair labor practices (ULPs) during the campaign or after the election, consequences follow, most of which lead to the union "winning" in whatever dispute that may be on the table.

As this is written new rules are in the offing that will make it much easier for union organizers to establish beachheads in targeted companies, accelerating the time currently taken to apply for and vote on union representation. Given the likelihood that these rules will become law, employers need to be even more aware of how their employees are perceiving the company (especially the way it's managed), and do all they can to create favorable impressions of the company in employees' eyes.

For Further Consideration

1. How do employees in your organization come to understand the policies and work rules that affect them? If you feel that improvement is needed in this area (the creation and administration of policies and work rules), what changes would you make? What would be some outcomes of these changes?

2. Can you recall a policy dispute that you were involved in? What was the issue, and how did the matter resolve itself? What lessons did you learn from the experience that will help you in similar situations in the future?

3. The Civil Rights Act came into being to "level the playing field" in the workplace and elsewhere. Has it been effective at doing so in your working life? Have you seen people in different protected categories receiving equal treatment? If not, what factors in your mind keep all of us from being more successful in terms of guaranteeing equal opportunity?

4. At organizations you have worked for, have you encountered an environment you'd describe as hostile— to one or more of the groups protected by the Civil Rights

Act? Did management act to improve those situations? In your mind, what could have been done to prevent them (the hostile environments) in the first place, and how successful were the efforts to fix them?

5. Have organizations you've worked for been covered under EO 11246?—the Executive Order requiring AAPs? If so, was your working life as a manager affected at all by this requirement? How was it affected? Do you see value in completing an AAP, beyond that of simple legal compliance? If so, what is that value?

6. In general, do you think our workplace culture may now be too careful when it comes to separating people from organizations? I.e., are we afraid to fire people? If this is true, is it (the fear) a good thing? How so? What about this situation could be counter-productive?

7. If your organization is union free and wants to stay that way, what concrete actions does the organization take to achieve that purpose? In your mind, how successful are these efforts? What, if anything, would you do differently to maintain the organization's union free status?

12 DISABILITY LAWS AND EMPLOYEE SAFETY

The Americans with Disabilities Act (ADA)

In the last chapter we talked about a level playing field in the workplace. What this means is the employment field should be "level" or equal for all those who want to play on it. This includes individuals with disabilities.

What you run into when you start examining various laws and regulations is the issue of definition. What the general public might mean by "disability," for example, may be different from the definition you find in the law—the Americans with Disabilities Act or ADA. For those of us in the workplace, in order to comply with the ADA, we need to know the definition of "disability" that we find there.

Those protected under the ADA are those who have a physical or mental impairment that "substantially limits" a so-called major life activity such as walking, working or caring for themselves. Also protected are those who are considered to have such an impairment, along with those who have had (or are thought to have had) that impairment in the past. In all likelihood you won't be asked to make the call as to whether or not a given individual meets the ADA's definition of "qualified individual with a disability"; the HR Department will eventually make that determination.

For our purposes in this book, our goal is to make you aware of compliance-related actions you may take that could prove problematic for your organization. In this regard, you may come into contact with individuals who do qualify for protection under the ADA, and you need to know what to do when that contact occurs.

We mentioned such an instance in the last chapter, when we talked about the woman who interviewed for a job—the person who had only one leg, whom you asked to demonstrate her ability to climb ladders. You didn't ask her about her condition, you simply asked her to demonstrate how she would perform one of the essential functions of the job.

Accommodation

You can't ask about a potentially disqualifying disability *before* a job offer is made. Once the offer is made, you can make start of work contingent upon passing a physical. Should that physical find a condition that could preclude the individual's employment, the issue of finding a reasonable accommodation could come up. The ADA asks that you enter into such a discussion in good faith, considering accommodations that do not involve an undue hardship for the organization. The latter are always decided on a case-by-case basis, and are often easy to implement—for several years after the ADA was enacted, the average cost of these accommodations was $500 or less.

Over time, existing employees can develop conditions that entitle them to protection under the ADA. When this occurs you shouldn't be the final arbiter of such an individual's status; that function goes to HR. You are the eyes and ears of HR, however, in the workplace; you are the one who needs to be aware of employees who might begin to struggle with tasks that were formerly handled in routine fashion. You may not be the one to initiate discussions about reasonable accommodations, but you need to be aware of the fact that the employee can ask for them. Should that happen, bad responses include outright refusals on your part to participate in the discussion, and/or entering into such discussions with no intent of changing the status quo. A good response is to listen attentively, then find a convenient time for the employee to discuss the issue with HR.

Perhaps the most important thing for you to remember is to not make *a priori* (before the fact) decisions about individuals who may be entitled to protection under the ADA. You can't, for example, elicit information from them that you later use to block a promotion, or, worse, to justify a separation from the organization. Remember the level playing field idea. Collectively and individually, individuals with disabilities have a great deal to offer in the workplace. We do both them and our organizations a disservice when we intentionally or unintentionally minimize that potential.

Be clear that you don't have to give people with disabilities the jobs or promotions they ask for. Under the law you have to give them equal *opportunities* to get them. It is always your prerogative to give the job or the promotion to the most qualified applicant.

ADA rules and definitions are complex, and they have changed substantially since the law was first enacted. To make sure you're dealing with the latest set of requirements, be sure to consult with legal counsel or your HR Department.

The Family and Medical Leave Act (FMLA)

Above we touched on the issue of definitions. When we begin to consider the Family and Medical Leave Act (FMLA), we run into that issue again. It would be convenient if the ADA and the FMLA had the same or a similar definition of whatever ailment, illness, injury or other condition qualified an individual for their respective protections—but such a common definition is not forthcoming.

ADA protections cover "physical or mental impairments." FMLA protections cover "serious health conditions," and the two definitions bear little resemblance to each other. Under the FMLA, such a serious condition is one that requires either inpatient medical care (in a hospital, hospice or residential care facility) or continuing treatment by a medical provider. The Act provides qualifying employees up to 12 weeks of unpaid leave to deal with a serious health condition. The

FMLA expands this coverage to a qualified employee's spouse, child or parent (a qualified employee is one who has worked for you for 12 months, with 1250 hours worked in the year preceding a given request for FMLA leave). If your company employs fewer than 50 employees within a 75 mile radius, those employees are not entitled to FMLA protection at all.

Requests for FMLA leave must go to HR. Paperwork must be completed and approval granted. Your involvement with FMLA can come in one of several ways. First, you need to recognize that qualified employees do have a right to the leave. If you are a department manager or business owner, you can't try to influence an individual not to take the leave, saying, for example, that he or she is needed at the moment, as it's the company's busy season. In a similar way, you can't engage in any sort of retaliatory action against an employee for exercising his/her legal rights under the FMLA.

And last (at least for our limited purposes in this book), you are the one who may need to monitor an employee's use of intermittent FMLA leave. This can be something of a nightmare, but the fact is that some serious health conditions do require periodic intervals of absence for treatment—either your employee's or the employee's spouse, child, or parent. The nightmare part includes tracking the amount of intermittent leave taken. The total amount of time available remains the same—12 weeks—but an individual is able to take that leave as the need arises, in intervals based on the smallest increments tracked in your company's pay system. Again, HR will manage the payroll dimensions of FMLA compliance; your role may be to receive requests for intermittent leave from an employee, then process specific requests for intervals of that leave as they arise.

Workers' Compensation (WC)

For a moment, let's remember our image of "inputs" coming at you during the course of your day. What we're trying to do is help you process those effectively. In the case of our compliance chapters, we want to minimize or avoid entirely any legal difficulty that might arise through your handling of those inputs. So far in this chapter, we've talked about your potential involvement with people protected under the ADA and the FMLA, and now we want to talk about a third issue involving your employees' health—the possibility that they may become ill, injured or even killed on the job. Should any of the latter occur, employees and their survivors are entitled to certain benefits under your state's Workers' Compensation ("Worker's Comp") laws.

Once again HR may be the department best able to help you in this area; if your organization has a Safety Manager, that individual will have primary responsibility for dealing with Workers' Comp issues. Your involvement will include ensuring that the proper paperwork is completed in a timely way following an accident, injury, or discovery of a work-related illness. These are Forms 300, 300A and 301, which your HR and/or Safety people will be familiar with, and which can be downloaded through OSHA's website.

Your other responsibility is for the overall safety of your people; in other words, you should be doing everything you can in cooperation with HR and Safety to preclude the need to initiate Worker's Comp programs (those that provide employees partial compensation, prescribe rules for potential partial employment, and outline procedures for employees' return to work following periods of recovery from work-related injuries).

You may be directly involved in periodic checks of employee recovery, but be guided by your HR and Safety people as to how "pushy" to be in these efforts. You may, in an effort to get a valuable employee back on the job quickly, inappropriately pressure him or her to return to work before he or she is really ready. This is more complex than it may seem. On the one hand you want to leave the individual's recovery in the hands of his/her doctor, but the company is also within its rights to ask for second and third opinions (from its own doctors), to ensure that the individual really needs the recovery time initially indicated. You should also be ready to explore opportunities for less rigorous work assignments the employee might perform. On the one hand this may comprise more work for you, but at least in these instances the company is getting some value from the employee while he/she recuperates.

The laws providing employees' absences from work due to medical issues comprise something of a swamp (one author referred to ADA, FMLA and WC rules as a "Bermuda Triangle"). For example, an employee injured on the job is of course entitled to WC benefits, but in the course of time it may become clear that he/she will never recover fully, and may thus qualify for protection under the ADA. Should the

175

latter occur, you may be involved in designing an accommodation for the individual. Still later, the employee's medical condition may require that he or she receive intermittent treatment—regardless of the accommodation you have provided—and the apparent "serious health condition" may require the intermittent treatment just mentioned (requiring leave) available under the FMLA. A Bermuda Triangle indeed.

You can't let this complexity obscure or reduce your responsibilities under each of these laws. Again, the best advice upon hearing of any kind of health-related issue is to ask HR, or, in the case of WC, your Safety people or legal counsel. These are the people best equipped to leap into this particular swamp with you.

The Occupational Safety and Health Act (OSHA)

The so-called OSH Act is administered by the Occupational Safety and Health Administration—also known familiarly as OSHA. Unless otherwise specified, we'll refer to OSHA in this latter light (that is, as the agency, not the law).

The agency's purpose is to ensure that people have safe places in which to work. The Act itself has regulations that include actual standards for the ways specific tasks must be performed, and these are included in designated sections of the Code of Federal Regulations (CFR). There are standards, for example, for confined space entry, for lockout/tag-out (which ensure that equipment is "de-energized" prior to being worked on), and for specific ways that hazardous chemicals are to be handled. The latter are articulated in the so-called Hazard Communication or "Hazcom" Standard, which stipulates that employees have a right to know which potentially hazardous chemicals are in the workplace, what the hazardous properties of these chemicals are, and how to remediate any exposures to them.

If your organization's hazcom program is less than robust, you may want to take the lead in strengthening it. I point out below that individual employees can contact OSHA, register complaints, and ask that OSHA make an onsite visit. The hazcom or Right to Know standard receives a lot of attention from the agency, and it is also one that affects virtually everyone in your workplace.

This is because hazardous substances can be found virtually anywhere, from cleaning closets, to shop floors to desk drawers (where white-out is often found). The hazcom standard requires that you identify every hazardous chemical in the workplace. It requires that you have on file so-called Material Safety Data Sheets (MSDSs) that contain all pertinent information about each chemical. Obtaining all of these can be somewhat daunting, as can organizing and making them available to your people as conveniently as possible. Daunting or not, it is a task that must be accomplished, not just for compliance purposes, but for the safety of everyone in the workplace.

Before I leave the hazcom standard, let me say a word about its labeling requirement. Chemicals in the workplace need to be labeled. I won't say this unconditionally, but many workplaces I've either worked in or visited have "holding" containers of various kinds, in which employees, either on their own or as instructed by superiors, "dump" various substances—often just to contain them and get them out of the way. Don't do this! Both OSHA and various environmental laws require that we identify, segregate, package, label and dispose of chemicals in tightly regulated ways. If you lack the resources to do this yourself, contact OSHA or an environmental services agency for assistance.

Where there is no specific standard, OSHA's so-called General Duty Clause comes into play, which says simply that it is our responsibility as employers to provide a safe and secure environment in which to work. If your organization is large enough, your Safety Manager, with your help, will ensure compliance with specific standards and with the General Duty Clause.

You should know that OSHA inspections can be requested by your employees, or the agency can decide on its own to visit your place of work. Following these inspections the inspectors will provide informal information as to what they've found, then send an official report of their findings. The agency will recommend any improvements it thinks necessary, and provide an interval within which those improvements should occur. Penalties for violations of OSHA standards depend on the number and severity of such violations, and whether the agency deems that they are willful or not. If they are found to be willful, penalties increase proportionately. In the event an individual is killed on the job due to willful disregard of an

OSHA standard, individuals in the organization become subject to criminal liability and imprisonment.

If you think the OSHA requirements and recommendations extend only to clearly hazardous workplaces such as mines and factories, think again. Accidents and injuries can occur anywhere, and the potential for these to occur on your watch must be continuously on your radar. Inputs of this type, in other words, come at you all the time, and you need to be sensitive to them. You might see, for example, too many extension cords plugged into one outlet; you may see boxes stacked precariously, ready to fall on someone; you may see an employee risking back injury through improper lifting procedures; you may see spills of various kinds waiting for people to slip in them—the list could go on and on.

Pay attention to these and similar inputs. Act on them when you see them.

For Further Consideration

1. What has been your experience in the workplace regarding individuals with disabilities? What is your basic attitude about that experience? Based on your experience, what guidance can you provide others in terms of optimizing the contributions of disabled individuals in the workplace?
2. Have people in your organization requested FMLA leave? If you have been involved at all in the administration of that leave, what has been your experience? Do you think it's easy for employees to abuse their rights to leave

under the FMLA? What abuses have you seen, and what do you recommend as measures to eliminate or reduce that abuse? What positive effects have you seen as individuals exercise their legal rights to this leave?

3. Workers' Comp insurance premiums depend in part on the number of employees you have, and also on your so-called use rate—the number of claims that have been filed against your organization over time. Do you know what your organization's rate is? Try to discover this information, and ask those in authority what you as an individual can do to reduce it. Even before seeking this information, what ideas do you have?

4. What are safety "hot spots" within your organization? That is, where do you think accidents and injuries are most likely to occur? What is being done now to mitigate them? What additional remedies could be applied?

5. What is the "safety climate" in your organization? How seriously do employees take measures to improve safety, to reduce the number of accidents and injuries that occur? What can you as an individual manager do to affect that culture?

6. Does your organization have a Hazcom or Employee Right to Know program? Ask stakeholders this question, being prepared to take the lead in either designing and developing such a program, or augmenting the existing one.

13 PRIVACY AND OTHER PROTECTIONS

Privacy

Do I need to remind you again about our purpose in this book? Okay. It's to make you aware of the full range of responsibilities you have as a manager, and to provide guidance as to how you can deal effectively and responsibly with those responsibilities. Please don't ask me to repeat that again.

In this chapter, I have to point out some responsibilities you have in regard to privacy: you have a many-sided obligation to keep your employees' personal information safe and secure; you have a similar obligation in regard to company information.

In regard to the first responsibility, issues arise when legitimate business concerns lead you to seek information about your employees outside of normal communication channels. What do you do, for example, if you suspect that an employee is dealing drugs from the workplace? Clearly you have a stake in ensuring that this kind of activity stops.

Do you go immediately to the "suspect's" locker and search it? Do you search the employee herself? Do you seize her computer?—Do you tap her phone, and/or intercept email communications she may be receiving?

First, I need to make my usual recommendation that you do none of the above as the Lone Ranger. You don't go riding into the above kinds of situations by yourself: you contact your manager, HR, Safety, Legal—before you do anything. Again, your primary function is to serve as eyes and ears, not as a vigilante committee of one.

Both statutory and common law cases have hinged on something called employee expectation of privacy. That means what it says. If employees have come to expect that you as management won't oversee a particular room, place, or device (which could include a desk), or body part, then a sudden breach of that practice could bring an invasion of privacy charge. The "for cause" principle, however, can override this expectation that employees may have. As in the example above, if you suspect drug dealing or theft, you have a right to investigate in ways outside of established practice.

Laws protect employees from some kinds of searches. Your HR rep can tell you about the Electronic Communications Privacy Act (ECPA) of 1986, which says in essence that you have no right to intercept electronic communications (e.g. emails) in transit; neither can you look into stored email (the first of these is dealt with in the Wiretap Act portion of the statute, and the second in the Stored Communication Act). The latter, however, doesn't have much "bite," in that if your company owns its own communications equipment, it has a right to monitor the information stored in that equipment (e.g. on its servers).

To return to our suspected drug dealer for a moment, you may say to yourself, "Let's set up a lie detector test for her!" Don't do that. I could go into this in detail, but let me condense my advice: don't do that. Another law, the Employee Polygraph Protection Act (EPPA) of 1988 makes it unlawful to use the results of such tests for employment purposes—except in a very narrow range of occupations. Just don't go there.

The best way to protect yourself from privacy-related complaints from employees is to develop a policy that says basically that they should have no expectation of privacy. Here is a portion of such a policy, produced by iWorkwell, Inc., in its article titled "Privacy in the Workplace: Protecting the Employer Without Violating Employee Rights":

> All the Organization's computers, networks, programs, computer files and electronic communications systems (including email, the Internet and Intranet, and any social media programs or sites used by the Organization for communication purposes) telephones and mobile phones have been acquired, installed and maintained at the Organization's expense. All these items are and will remain the sole property of the Organization. All these items are intended to be used for business purposes.

Any employee using the Organization's equipment must be aware that the Organization retains the right to monitor the use of the equipment and to inspect the equipment at any time, without notice. The Organization may review computer usage, telephone usage and mobile phone usage, without notice.

The Organization may retrieve, read and disclose any information, voice mail and electronic mail on its equipment at any time and without notice. The Organization may also search any other Organization property, such as desks, vehicles, cabinets and other storage areas at any time and without notice.[1]

Protecting Employee Information

The second part of your responsibility in regard to employee privacy is to protect your employees' personal information. As you know, identity theft is rampant, and once people come to work for you, you have a duty to ensure that their personal information (e.g. health-related information, Social Security Numbers, immigration status) is kept secure.

If you have an HR Department, your HR people will have protocols in place for protecting employees' health-related information (as required, for example, by the Health Insurance Portability and Accountability Act—HIPAA—of 1996). Medical information of all kinds must be kept secure and separate from personnel files, the principle being that none of that information should be accessible to those making employment decisions. As mentioned previously, nothing should be in a personnel file that someone could use for discriminatory purposes.

Please take this issue seriously. Monitor the workplace to see if employee information is accessible—on computer screens, in open files, on individuals' desks—and take steps to ensure that that information is properly secured. If HR does not currently have a specific policy in place to ensure compliance in this area, ask that it develop one with all speed.

Protecting Company Information

Virtually all people in an organization—management person-nel in particular—have access to company information. Much of this information is proprietary (i.e. it is the sole property of the organization), and part of your responsibility in regard to privacy is to make sure that sensitive company information is not disclosed.

Your company, for example, may have developed manufacturing processes that give it a major edge over its competitors. Any information about these processes needs to be protected, whether it be in the form of equipment specifications, production reports, control system schematics or employee training material. Access to any of that and similar information could be highly desirable to competitors.

Financial reports comprise another kind of highly sensitive information. These reports provide snapshots of where an organization is financially, and competitors could use them to discover information such as which markets your company is targeting, as well as which expense categories may be over or under budget. The latter could be useful in a competitor's own financial projections.

Social media sites such as LinkedIn and Facebook provide an avenue for the potential sharing of sensitive company information. Your company should have a policy in place governing who can post such information, as well as specifying what can be posted and what can't. As a country and as a society we're still deciding many things that are permissible and those that aren't in this area (Al Gore, after all, just did invent the internet not long ago), so be careful. Share any policy and work rule changes in this area with legal counsel before you go public with them.

Again, your task is to be the person on the floor (or on the internet, as in the case of material appearing in social media), the one who can spot the inappropriate sharing of company information. Individuals responsible for this unauthorized "leaking" of information need to be identified and subjected to appropriate discipline.

<u>Away From the Workplace</u>

What your employees do away from the workplace is their business, right? Yes and no. You have a legitimate right to restrict some employee behavior away from the workplace, but employees also have considerable freedom to act as they please when they're away from the workplace, on their own.

Employees are not free, for example, to engage in activities that involve conflicts of interest. If they engage in behavior that is not in the best interests of you as their employer, you have a right to ask them to cease and desist that behavior. For example, if your company provides certain services (let's say you operate a janitorial business), and your employee offers a client a thirty percent reduction in the fee you're charging for services, that would clearly be a conflict of interest, and you could discipline your employee appropriately for doing that.

Do employees need to behave responsibly at company-sponsored events? Can't they let their hair down and do as they please at these functions? What if, for example, you provide alcohol, Alex from Accounting has several too many, and gets into an accident driving home from the function? Your liability in this instance increases—as the sponsor of the event and as the entity that provided the alcohol (in quantities that Alex wasn't able to handle responsibly).

Surely, you can keep your employees from participating in political events sponsored by hate groups of various kinds? Here the area gets a bit grey. Certainly you could object if an employee were to wear a company uniform or display a company logo at such an event, which would suggest that you as the employer endorse policies of the sponsoring organization. You can also have general policy provisions about harassment and any kind of discriminatory activity, should these be in evidence at, say, a rally sponsored by a white supremacy group. Other than these kinds of restrictions, however, employees enjoy considerable freedom to be where they choose to be and do what they choose to do away from the workplace.

Here's another rather homely example (in the sense of being common or familiar). What if your company sponsors a bowling team? Of course everyone in the league knows that they're your employees, as your logo is splashed all over their red and yellow bowling shirts (I know I'm going to receive charges that I'm prejudiced against bowlers and bowling in general, and that is absolutely not true). To continue, what if it's a mixed league—meaning teams are comprised of both men and women—and members of the team (perhaps Alex is a bowler too, and once again loses some self control) make loud, suggestive, objectionable remarks of a sexual nature to members of another team?

You can restrict that kind of behavior. It perhaps violates your company's stated vision, mission and "credo," as well as your harassment and discrimination policies. It reflects badly on your organization in the eyes of the community; it damages your reputation.

As I just mentioned, beyond these kinds of restrictions, your employees have considerable freedom away from the workplace. They do, after all, have freedom of speech and freedom of assembly. As long as they are not breaking the law through their participation at events that you personally and as a company find objectionable, they are pretty much off limits in terms of your ability to control them.

We said in our first compliance-related chapter that you should let policies do your heavy lifting in terms of regulating employee behavior. In this area especially—conduct away from the workplace—it would be advisable to write down exactly what your policy guidelines are. By all means have legal counsel review those policies, as not only are the various restrictions and protections a bit on the murky side, but counsel will know the specific local and state regulations that apply, and these vary widely from state-to-state, even county-to-county.

Wage and Hour Requirements

HR and Payroll are the departments having primary responsibility to ensure that the wage and hour laws are honored in your organization, but you own a piece of this responsibility as well.

People working in so-called "nonexempt" positions are subject to minimum wage and overtime rules. "Nonexempt" means what it says, that people working in this classification aren't exempt from these requirements. You need to pay them at least the prevailing minimum wage, and you need to pay them time-and-a-half when they work more than 40 hours in a given workweek.

Your role as a supervisor or manager in this area is first of all to identify jobs correctly as exempt vs. nonexempt. And not to sound like a broken record, but HR will oversee this process, hopefully making sure that your organization's classifications are correct.

As for your part, what you may be tempted to do is classify someone as exempt in an effort to save the overtime premium. You don't even want to know the consequences for misclassifying people in this way. The government is REALLY interested in collecting its due when it comes to payroll taxes. If you pay someone less than you should, classifying them as exempt, you pay less in total. The wage and hour people consider this cheating the government out of its due, and they really hate it.

Those exempt from the overtime requirements include so-called "white collar" employees such as executives, administrative employees, and professionals. Outside sales people and business owners are also classified as exempt. With some exceptions, those occupying highly technical positions can also qualify as exempt; again, your HR people will know these exceptions and distinguishing factors.

As for your personal involvement in this area, you may also be tempted from time to time to engage in the following (and you shouldn't):

- Asking people to punch out, then return to finish a project. All time worked needs to be acknowledged and paid.
- Avoiding the overtime requirement by claiming that it was unauthorized; if the employee works the overtime hours, he or she needs to be paid, authorization or no.
- Asking people to perform job-related duties on their own time, e.g. dropping off mail or running other errands.
- Classifying break or meal time as non-paid; the wage and hour people think that breaks of between 5 and 20 minutes constitute work time, and that time must be paid.

<u>Immigration</u>

People working in your organization must have a legal right to do so. Under provisions of the Immigration Reform and Control Act (IRCA) of 1986, employees must demonstrate that they have a legal right to work in this country by filling out IRCA's Form I-9, on which they certify that they have this right. HR will oversee this process, visually inspecting required documents that verify the employee's right to work in this country.

You do know, don't you, that citizenship status is not a valid, legal criterion to use in making employment decisions about people? Non-US citizens are entitled to protection under the Civil Rights Act and other discrimination-related statutes, as long as they can furnish appropriate documentation of their right to work in this country (e.g., their possession of the appropriate visa or permit).

If you're involved at all in the storage and maintenance of employee records (and you shouldn't be, except perhaps for such things as production reporting and other department-specific documents), remember that Form I-9 needs to be kept isolated from other employee records. Our earlier principle governs this practice: no one who makes employment decisions regarding an individual should have access to information he or she could use in a discriminatory manner. Form I-9 can include this kind of information (e.g. country of origin information that appears on a passport), and therefore must be kept in its own secure location.

Record Keeping

The rules describing which employee records must be kept, for how long, under what conditions and to which speci-fications—are many and complex. You need to ask your HR people about this.

What I want you to do is survey your work area and determine what kinds of employee information you may be keeping. What I really hope you don't find are notes you may have taken during interviews with prospective candidates, both internal and external candidates. The information you find may be electronic or hard copy, but what I don't want those notes to say are things like:

- "Age? Ability to handle line speed?"
- "Too many women in the department already."
- "Being from India, won't fit in with redneck element."
- "Gut tells me no."
- "Worry about criminal record, but think he's learned his lesson."

In the event of a complaint, these kinds of notes are discoverable (we made this point in Chapter Eleven). You understand the difficulty with these kinds of statements, don't you? For one thing they indicate an inclination to discriminate. For another, they suggest a sloppy employee selection process (one in which gut feelings can predominate), and in the last example, they could reveal a potential negligent hire situation. What you would be saying, in the last bullet, is that you suspect an individual could bring harm to the workplace, but you choose to employ that individual anyway.

Your organization should control personnel files, both access to them, who can take them out of their respective file drawers, and for how long. The last thing I would want to see is a stack of these files on your desk—especially if you're not sitting at your desk. The information in those files should be accessible only to those with a legitimate need to examine them.

Be careful with all employee-related information. Don't keep it if you have no reason to. You can have department files on your people, but restrict the kind of information you keep in those files: it can be names, addresses and phone numbers; it can be schedules and assignments; it can even be records of attendance and disciplinary matters. But keep it "clean," free of anything of a personal, cultural or medical nature that could be used in a discriminatory manner.

We said starting into these last three chapters that the workplace is something of a legal minefield, one that you need to navigate with care. Please understand that we have only scratched the surface in these three chapters, that there's much to learn and remember in this area (laws, regulations, and compliance). Our chapters in this and other areas are "awakeners" and thought starters, not definitive information or final answers. The Compliance Screen on your filter is one to watch; it is always going to be something of a moving target. The legal "pond" is one you don't want to swim in alone. Get those HR, Safety and Legal people to jump in there with you. And good luck.

For Further Consideration

1. Do your employees have expectations that their privacy will be respected in the workplace? On what do you base your answer? Have you been involved in privacy-related disputes? What were the resolutions in those disputes?
2. Do you use surveillance cameras to monitor your workplace(s)? Could placements of these cameras constitute a violation of employees' reasonable expectation of privacy?
3. How does your company protect the privacy of employee information? Have instances occurred where these expectations were violated?—i.e., discovery was made that sensitive employee information was compromised? What was done to prevent this from recurring?
4. Does your organization have a presence on social media sites? Who is responsible in this area? Are any controls in place as to what kind of information is appropriate for posting on these sites?
5. Are you comfortable with the pay systems operating in your organization? Are you ever questioned by your people as to why certain hours weren't paid?—and how did you respond in these instances?
6. What is the employee demographic in your department, or in your organization as a whole, and are you sure that everyone in your workforce has a legal right to be there?

7. Describe your record keeping procedures. What organizational strategies do you use for your employee records, and can you see any room at all for improvement? What procedures might you change?

8. Identify any additional legal issues that affect you, that weren't addressed in the compliance chapters and share them with your HR people. Working with them, how can you improve your overall compliance performance?

Notes

1. Johnson, Melissa et.al. "Privacy in the Workplace: Protecting the Employer Without Violating Employee Rights." www.iWorkwell.com Copyright © 2001-2011 iWorkwell, Inc. Quoted with permission.

14 MANAGING AND TECHNOLOGY

<u>The Fact of Life</u>

We deal with technology all the time, both at home, when we travel, and when we go to work. We are all much smarter with it (much of the time out of necessity) than we give ourselves credit for being. Even yours truly has solved minor computer problems. I'll admit that these are usually in the "Is it turned on?" category, but I've dealt with them nonetheless.

Here's the actual definition of technology: it's the practical application of knowledge. That means we can use or apply our knowledge of something (something such as electricity or a riding mower) to solve a problem or achieve a result. "Technology" refers to both the application of knowledge itself, and the overall *capability* and related skill(s) of making the application happen.

Technology at Work

Each of us is already a technological person. As such we have the ability to understand and use new technologies as those present themselves to us. Here is a succession of writing technologies that I've mastered: I've gone from crayon to pencil to pen to manual typewriter to electric typewriter to word processor. Those are word-into-manuscript technologies, and I can also use various document management technologies.

Think for a moment about the technologies that affect your life in the workplace. We now have forklifts in warehouses that drive themselves. We have bar codes and their related technologies. Our pay appears in our bank accounts magically (I still don't see how they squeeze checks through those wires). But by far the most pervasive technologies that affect us in the workplace are related to information technology or IT. What we've become astonishingly good at is configuring, moving, storing and delivering information electronically.

This has transformed work and will continue to do so at warp speed. In the face of this, it seems to me that we have two choices. First, we can pretend that it isn't happening, and cling to knowledge applications, processes and procedures that we're familiar with and feel comfortable using. This is ostrich-with-head-in-sand thinking. Or, second, we can accept the fact that the transformation is occurring, will continue to occur, and try as hard as we can to keep up. The implications of picking which of these trains we want to ride are pretty stark. I think we need to try to keep up.

As with the other dimensions of our jobs, the way we "see" ourselves in relation to technology is critical. If we see ourselves as dinosaurs in this realm, then that's what we'll be (and we recall what happened to the dinosaurs). I'll admit that I do this (refer to myself as a dinosaur). This can be a copout and an excuse to remain where we are—and again, color me "guilty" in this area. We sometimes inject humor as a way to deflect attention away from the fear we feel— perhaps fear that we just won't be able to catch on at all or we won't be able to catch up. We remember what President Roosevelt said about this: the real thing to fear is fear itself, not a real or imagined bogeyman of some sort.

As for technology (I just refused to refer to it as the "technology bogeyman"), the only differences between me and Mark Zuckerberg (the Facebook guy), are ones of degree, not of kind. I'm somewhat older than he is for example. I'm somewhat less knowledgeable than he is, at least in some areas (I may know more about the Chicago Cubs than he does). And I possess somewhat fewer skills than he has to work with highly technical matters affecting information technology. Could I bridge the latter gaps in skill and technology? I absolutely could, given world enough and time.

So I'm recommending that you try what may be a new perception, a new frame of reference, in regard to technology itself, and to *yourself* as one who interacts with technology. That frame of reference is that technology is a subject that we already know about and work with, and further, that as new developments occur in it, we can learn and work with those as well. End of story.

Some Disclaimers

Now you do need to keep your wits about you. I don't want to devote precious space here to the "dark sides" of the technological age we live in, but they are certainly here:

- We can get too absorbed with new technological artifacts that emerge, perhaps becoming glued to iPhones and iPads, and in the process failing to develop needed interpersonal skills. We can lose our ability to relate face-to-face.
- We can be texting in our cars and crash into telephone poles.
- Technological innovations come so quickly that they can't all be saviors of civilization as we understand it—in other words, we still need to apply discernment, sometimes waiting at least a week to see if a given application will do all it says it will do.
- We can't throw established, proven methods out just because they are that—established. There's that saying about something that ain't broke.
- We need to be aware of the anxiety that can arise over our failure to learn about and acquire the newest thing. When that gets too intense, we have to forget, at least for a while, about acquiring that newest thing.
- We can have what amounts to blind faith in technology, sometimes ignoring the natural laws and rhythms that have stood the planet in fairly good stead over the past zillion years or so. The universe was sort of well-engineered from its inception; we can forget sometimes

that perhaps our attempts to improve upon it through technology may be neither necessary nor desirable. We can't let ourselves get out of synch with Mother Nature, losing sight of all She's given us.

My goal early in this chapter is to prepare the ground for a somewhat more serious discussion of technology. While I want you to become more comfortable with both the subject and with your ability to work more compatibly with it, there are several key facts we need to keep in mind (in addition to the "don't mess with Mother Nature" comments just made).

A valued client made some excellent points about how IT matters can be experienced in the workplace. He reminded me that IT can be "handed off" to those not specifically trained to handle it. Since these people are often "can-do" kinds of people, they hurl themselves into their roles with sometimes mixed results. The advice is to simply watch this tendency, realizing that while I'm trying to make the subject of technology approachable in this chapter, we do need to keep its true nature in mind. It has its complexities, and it changes at dizzying speed. When we assign a technological function to someone, we need to stand ready to help that individual with more expert assistance should he or she run into trouble. File this in your "Don't Let Stan Flounder" folder.

A second point my client made was that technical people are not always the most engaging communicators among us. They tend to see things in terms of blacks and whites, not shades of grey. My client's advice was to pay attention to the communication issues your "techies" may have with their non-specialist colleagues (such as *moi*), who live in a somewhat greyer universe. Remember too that techies are often not the most patient people; they want us to grasp things as quickly as they do, and we just don't.

Finally, he told me to be aware that resolving technological issues can take time. When I have a computer issue here in my large and sumptuous suite of offices (you are to smile knowingly when you read that, understanding that I don't have a sumptuous suite of offices), I expect my "computer guy" to be here instantly, troubleshoot the issue(s) instantly, and have me up and running again instantly. This is asking a lot. You expect your technical people to keep everything running (and everyone working) while troubleshooting and fixing what can be highly complex problems. And remember the communication issue just described. The techie (Mr. or Ms. Black and White) is working with the Greys as he/she tries to understand and solve a given issue. We need to give our technical people the time they need, and we need to cut them a lot of slack.

Information Technology

As I mentioned earlier, information technology (IT) is that dimension of technology that may have the greatest impact on you—this is that capacity for configuring, moving, storing and delivering information that I alluded to. It may be instructive to remind ourselves of how these processes used to be handled.

Much of the information we needed was packaged in books (and still is, I hasten to point out). We put the books in libraries, and librarians help us access the information in those books. We used to have hardbound encyclopedias, and people made reasonably good livings selling them (the encyclopedias did, after all, need to be updated, and people needed to buy the updated versions). In our libraries a technological breakthrough occurred when we learned how to film text pages, putting their images onto microfiche (sheets) and microfilm (rolls), the better to store them (saving floor space in libraries).

In former times, we found books in the library by going to the card catalog and to an index of periodical literature to find articles. Computers make this much simpler now. In the "old days," however, if you were doing a research assignment, often you would use index cards to record publication information on each of the works you needed to cite, and also to write down key pieces of information from your sources. A cumbersome, labor-intensive, time-consuming process.

Now of course we have computers and the internet. Information is available to us in seconds, and it's available in great quantity. It's delivered to us in a variety of ways, through a variety of media, tools and applications (iPhones, laptops, programs or "aps"). Success in your position may depend on your ability to access needed information quickly, in forms that you can understand and make understandable to others.

As this is written (this is another way of saying that it's already obsolete), one development that's occurring in the technological universe is cloud computing. While it's no longer new, this development is having and will have enormous impact on IT generally. It provides us with a useful example of how we learn about and absorb new technological information.

In my extremely fragile understanding, cloud computing in its simplest form refers to the accessing of both data, software and IT infrastructure through the internet—vs. acquiring and using these individual components in dedicated, "physical" (vs. simulated or "virtual") computing environments. An example of such a physical, mechanical process is loading MS Office applications onto your personal PC. Many of you work in companies that have dedicated IT infrastructure— "dedicated" to serving the IT needs of the organization—and this "infrastructure" includes pilgrims who will come to your work station and actually load up new software and other components for you as you need them. My suite of offices depends on Josh the Computer Guy.

The way IT functions may operate for you is that dedicated servers of the infrastructure receive individual requests from people throughout your organization. The servers process those requests "in house," and deliver the appropriate services and data back to individual users. Allegedly, cloud computing saves both hardware costs and time by "bundling" all of the foregoing (infrastructure, software and data) into perhaps a company-specific, private "cloud" which individual users can access directly through the internet. The cloud people like to compare accessing IT services through a cloud to what we do now with electrical power. We don't often go to the expense of building our own power plants to serve the needs of our organizations. Rather, we pay someone a "subscription" to access the service (power) from the power company. This is what many of us will do eventually through cloud computing.

Here is my point in presenting this brief discussion of cloud computing. The first fact is, I just learned about it recently. And as brief and possibly inaccurate as my account of it may be, I think I basically "get it." The exposure I've had to the concept has given me enough of a platform upon which to base further learning. I not only kind of "get" cloud computing now; I am confident that I can learn more.

Given the speed at which new information can appear, we need to keep something else in mind: we each need to take the time required to learn new things. There are no shortcuts and there is no magic; we either take the time required to learn something or we don't learn it! Most people won't fault us for ignorance; they may fault us for pretending, for suggesting that we know more than we really know.

Dr. Scott Peck gave a great example of the "time taking" phenomenon. Out for a walk, he encountered a neighbor working on a power mower. The neighbor had the mower apart, and was deeply into his task. Dr. Peck watched for a moment, then said, "I could never do that." The neighbor didn't respond for a moment, then replied, "That's because you don't take the time."

I see so much truth and wisdom in that response. I'm unclear how we've arrived at this "I need to understand this immediately" point of view, but that's where I think we are. We are smart, capable people. We can do virtually anything we set our minds to, but we need to remember that computers, programs and lawn mowers are *complicated*! Of course we need to give ourselves some time to assess and solve problems that arise with them.

We can forget that new phenomena do appear in our lives (microwave ovens for example), and that when they do, we have to "pick up" and use information and terminology associated with them. We also had to learn, for example, what air bags were. Then we had to learn something about what they were designed to do, picking up related information and terminology in the process. That's all it ever is: new stuff, related information and terminology.

I also want you to remember the library example above, and put that next to the information about cloud computing. In both examples we're talking about the configuring, moving, storing and delivering of information. One methodology handles the foregoing in a hands-on, physical manner, the other does so electronically. Do we need to understand every nuance of how the latter methodology (the cloud kind) goes about its work? I hope not! Is a kind of global, general inkling of how it goes about that work interesting and potentially desirable? Absolutely.

Remember, you are a *manager* in what is probably a technologically robust environment. You are expected to achieve results in that environment—not just through your interaction with the people who populate the area, but with the physical and virtual elements that reside there with you. You have to "interface" with the latter, to use an IT term we probably all know. The more you can approach these current and future interfaces with courage, humility and confidence, the better.

The Automated Workplace

As a manager you oversee increasing automation of work processes. We've already discussed one important implication of this fact, and that is the role of IT generally as it supports data management in organizations. But you face automation in the workplace generally, and this means the potential replacement of people in many instances by machines and computers. How everyone responds in these instances has important implications for the ongoing health and prosperity of the organization.

Depending of course on the organization, you may be expected to participate in the automating of the workplace generally. By this time most of us know about lean manufacturing, whose primary tenet is the creation (manufacturing or processing) and delivery of goods and services, utilizing the minimum of resources required— delivered "just in time."

Sometimes this involves changing the "footprint" of the manufacturing or processing floor, eliminating as much redundancy, complexity, time and waste as possible. Clearly if you manage in an environment that implements this approach, you'll be expected to understand it, help with its ongoing implementation, and recommend changes as those occur to you. Once again there should be nothing inherently intimidating in this process; it's another instance in which we can apply our basic questions: What is it? How does it work? What terms do we need to learn in order to work with it successfully?

An added factor, however, is the important communication you need to have with the people involved when changes of this kind (automation) occur. You need to make the changes understandable (if not actually palatable) to the people affected, assisting in many instances in retraining or in finding appropriate transfers for people. You need a multiple focus when this happens: a desire to see the organization be as efficient and productive as possible; a willingness to see the potential in people to take on and master new tasks; and the ability to communicate both of the foregoing to the people whose lives are affected. And you remember of course the additional communication issues that can arise between your technical people and the "others." You may be called upon to be the interpreter and the intermediary between people in both these categories should failures to communicate occur.

You can do it. You just need to take the time.

I realize that there are dimensions of technology I haven't touched on. I realize as well that it is one of the most important dimensions of your job as a manager. If there are qualities I could recommend that you work on as you approach the technology dimension generally, they would be these: open-mindedness, agility, perspective, patience and compassion. Let me say just a word about each.

- You need to be open-minded in the sense that positive change—most likely technological in nature—has already come and that much more is barreling toward you. Among the new things may be those that can lead to a better life for you and the people who work for you. Be open to that.

- Agility means that you have the wherewithal to change course and take action quickly, not being bound by "analysis paralysis" or similar malady—perhaps a need for things to be perfect before you try them.

- Cultivate a sense of perspective. Remember who you are and what's important to you, and apply this to your department and organization as well. Refuse to be stampeded. Whatever you're doing now must be working reasonably well; don't leap on the Change Just Because It's Change bandwagon.

- Be patient with yourself and with your people. Give all of you the time needed to understand and master the changes that have already come and that will come. Be ready to perform your role as intermediary. Take the time you need.

- Remember that success in your organization depends on the people who work there. Have compassion for them and what they face day-to-day; learn how to express this compassion in real, unaffected ways.

I mentioned earlier something that happened to me on my regular train ride to Philadelphia—it was when I came across the Mark Zuckerberg article. When I go to Philadelphia I work all day in a large office building. When I get on the elevator at the end of the day, I see what to me is an amazing phenomenon.

When people get on the elevator, they're already staring at their cell/smart phones. They're already attached to someone outside their physical environment. There is no eye contact; all eyes are on the phones.

When I ask people in classes to put phones away, you'd think I was asking for an organ transplant. People get the shakes when asked to give up their phones, even for a little while. To me this is pitiful, counter-productive, and limiting. The commercials we see as this is written often depict people staring at their phones, pleased that they have the fastest ones available. They're just sitting there, staring at the phones. If this is life, it's life that is myopic, sterile, and debilitating.

We need to remember that the most meaningful contact between human beings occurs face to face. We as *homo sapiens* are the most exotic, complicated, irreducibly complex entities ever created. *We* are; not machines. We need to pay attention to one another's humanity, remembering our basic nature, which is flesh, blood, emotion, intellect and spirit. We need to communicate with words and sentences, face-to-face and eye-to-eye.

Remember to put the phone down sometimes; actually look at people and talk to them.

For Further Consideration

1. Look at the technological "progression" cited early in this chapter about writing—about the movement from crayon to word processor. Can you cite similar progressions? What has happened, for example, in the realm of automotive technology? How has technology affected travel in general?
2. In your experience, how has technology affected your working life? Describe in particular how technology has affected the processes used to perform work (think, for example of phone service, and of automation generally).
3. Have people in organizations you've worked for (past and present) divided themselves according to their knowledge of information technology? In other words, are there individuals or groups who consider themselves "in the know," vs. those who aren't? Do you think such distinctions are real? What are the implications associated with seeing people in this way?
4. How has technological change been introduced into the organizations you've worked for? Have the methods used been effective? In hindsight, how would you have changed them? Have you ever mediated a "Techie vs. Non-Techie" issue? How did that work out?

5. How are people in your workplace adjusting to technological change? How have you helped them adjust? If some are not adjusting well, can you think of additional ways you can help them?

6. Look again at the "disclaimer" section of this chapter. Can you think of additional "watchouts" we might consider in regard to technology? What are they? If your organization has "handed off" technology to someone not specifically trained in the field, how is that person doing? Can you think of additional ways that you can be of help and support?

7. What is the next technological change you see coming— that will affect the way you work? How are you preparing for it?

8. Has automation occurred in your organization? How was that change accommodated? What are the current effects of it? If these are in any way negative, can you think of ways to counteract them?

9. How do you feel about your possession and expression of our five key qualities?—open-mindedness, agility, perspective, patience and compassion? If you could identify one for further development, which would it be?

15 RISK: IT CAN HAPPEN HERE

Categories of Risk

Risk management is a field of study all its own—several fields actually. It can apply specifically to measures business owners take to preserve their investments in their companies, ensuring that orderly succession occurs should anything happen to them. It can also apply to investments, referring to ways that people spread investment risk in their portfolios— so they won't get hurt too badly should a given segment of those portfolios perform badly. We're taught to diversify holdings, to put whatever eggs we have in different baskets.

We'll talk briefly about one of these kinds of risks later (succession planning), but mainly discuss risk in the context of dealing with the unexpected. We've stressed the importance of planning throughout this book, and maybe this seems like we're going in another direction—but if you recall, back in Chapter Five, we did have that one screen labeled "Screaming Crises." An emergency situation of whatever kind can develop quickly into one of those. We recall how that "crisis" screen expanded when Captain Sullenberger first saw that something was terribly wrong with his airplane. When something like this happens, we as managers must be ready to minimize whatever damage may occur.

Thinking the Unthinkable

I remember how beautiful the day was, driving to work the morning of September 11, 2001. The sky was deep blue, the air was clear and clean—a simply spectacular September morning here in the Northeast. Of course, that day was to become memorable for very different reasons, reasons related to airplanes crashing into buildings and into the ground, related to thousands of people dying in those crashes.

I've said on at least a couple of occasions in this book that we're not in Kansas anymore. Let me make that clear again, and underline it, in this chapter. The terrorist attacks of September 11, if not the cause of our departure from Kansas, are certainly a major symbol of that fact. The world we live in is not the one many of us grew up in.

That was a world in which people didn't lock their doors. A world in which war didn't come to the shores of our country. A world in which teenaged boys didn't bring guns to their school in Columbine, Colorado and murder their teachers and classmates. In the world we live in now, a man, just this last weekend, entered a hair salon in Huntington Beach, California, and shot to death his wife and seven other people.

On September 11, 2001, there were CEOs, managers and supervisors on all floors of each World Trade Center tower. In their wildest dreams, none had conceived of what transpired on that day. The same could be said of the teachers and administrators at Columbine High School on the day those attacks occurred, and the same could be said of the salon proprietor in Huntington Beach. As much as all of us wish this weren't true, we can no longer pretend—and wish—that these kinds of events had never occurred, nor that they won't occur again.

Paying Attention

If you've been a manager long enough, you will have dealt with a dangerous situation. I worked in a plant in which a man walked in through security with a baseball bat and attacked a man on an upper floor whom he suspected of having an affair with his wife. I've received a call from a solid waste worker alleging that his immediate superior was carrying a gun. Another day I *found* a gun in a first line supervisor's desk drawer.

For all of us who manage, my first and perhaps most important words are "Wake up." The potential for violence—since indeed we've moved out of Kansas—is real. You as someone with responsibility in and for the workplace, again have to be the eyes and ears of your organization, staying alert for anything that seems out of the ordinary or suspicious. Further, you also have to respond as effectively as possible when unforeseen and potentially dangerous incidents occur.

Reading about the incident in Huntington Beach, people at the salon in which the murders occurred certainly knew of difficulty between the wife and her estranged husband. In fact, several people actually heard the husband threatening his wife in the salon just days before the shooting. In a prolonged custody dispute with her husband, she had expressed fear for her safety multiple times in the days and weeks that preceded the incident. The fear turned out to be very well-founded.

Perhaps nothing could have been done to prevent this act by a clearly unbalanced person, but at least we should learn from the incident to pay attention and take precautions when we see and hear actual threats of violence. Police could have been made aware of the threats—especially those that had actually been made in the salon—and perhaps they could have intervened in some way.

With 20-20 hindsight, we remember the flying lessons taken by the September 11 attackers in our country; we remember the fertilizer and explosive purchases made by Timothy McVey before he blew up the Alfred P. Murrah Federal Building in Oklahoma City. We need to have eyes to see and ears to hear, as much as possible developing what could be called 20-20 *fore*sight.

Responding to Incidents

I worked for a time in the hazardous waste industry. In that environment, we were all trained to be ready for the unexpected, especially for incidents involving potentially dangerous releases of chemicals, explosions and fires. Every year, to comply with a legal/operating permit requirement, all of us had to extinguish a fire properly, using the fire extinguisher appropriate to the specific kind of fire presented to us.

So within our specific environment it was easy to see that trained people would be needed should an emergency develop (we would see these screaming warning labels on drums of hazardous waste, for example). We had dedicated teams of first responders, ready to leap into action as needed. These people were sometimes not the actual managers in the organization, but those who volunteered to take on leadership roles in the event of an emergency. If your organization is large enough and/or particularly susceptible to incidents of various kinds, you may want to develop such a system.

At our facility, when an incident occurred on any shift, alarms would sound and the people trained to respond would take over. They were trained in what to do, and each had people in each processing area of the facility who were trained and ready to respond in their respective areas.

Their duties were to communicate with one another; to assess the size and nature of the threat that was occurring; to ensure that people were assisted to areas of safety (all of us knew which areas we were to assemble in in the event of an emergency); to assist anyone who may have been injured; to conduct immediate operations to contain and restrict damage; and to summon additional aid as needed.

The foregoing could be the outline of an emergency response plan for any organization. What is to be avoided is Chicken With Its Head Cut Off Syndrome, which is what occurs when no plan at all is in place to deal with an emergency. The idea is to think of what to do before something bad happens, not *while* something bad is happening (this is why organizations conduct fire drills).

Recent events teach us that it's not a question anymore of *whether* an emergency is going to develop, it's *when* one will develop. So when an emergency occurs, what do we do?

First, we can do as much in the way of prevention as possible, as much in advance as possible. Let's talk first about emergencies involving people harming others in the workplace. We can develop zero tolerance for violence policies, train people in them and enforce them rigorously. If involved in employee selection, we can ensure that all diligence is followed in terms of background checks. If we see aggressive behavior of any kind in the workplace (even threatening looks), we confront it and keep it from recurring. If employees express fear—perhaps of a spouse—we take such expressions seriously, offering whatever resources are available through the company, and alerting management and security of the situation.

All of the foregoing dovetail into the general consideration of knowing who our employees are. If we know who they are, we pick up readily on signs of worry or agitation. We're not psychologists, perhaps we're not even friends, but our responsibility is to be alert for any sign that something isn't right with someone, to make appropriate inquiry, and be prepared to offer resources that can help.

Should an incident involving a violent person actually begin, your first responsibility is to secure the safety of as many people as possible, assisting them to find cover or means of escape from the area, while minimizing the potential danger to yourself. You weren't hired to be a security person or a bouncer, so remember we're talking about reasonable measures here. In most cases, should you decide to confront a deranged person who has a weapon, the outcome for you will not be a good one.

Whatever the situation, someone needs to stay calm. If you are in charge, perhaps all you can do is call your own security people and/or 911, and take whatever cover you can find. Both of these actions could prove valuable in an emergency.

For other kinds of emergencies, you need to plan for them, perhaps creating the kind of emergency response team described above. In organizations of any size, people need to know how to get out of a building in the event of a fire or explosion. If you are in an area susceptible to natural disasters such as hurricanes, floods, or tornadoes, you need to determine what to do should you find yourself in harm's way. Name someone in the organization Emergency Response Coordinator, and give that person the time and resources needed to put together an Emergency Response Plan. Once that plan is in place, train everyone in the organization in what their responsibilities are should it become necessary to implement the plan.

After incidents like those described above, managers need to assist with damage control in whatever ways they can. This means helping secure the area from any additional damage, and seeing as much as practicable to the physical and emotional needs of the people who've been affected. Arrange for counseling and other services for those affected in the weeks following an incident. Rather than trying to forget that it ever happened, give people the opportunity to talk.

Other Security Threats

Your organization is a living entity, one whose life can be threatened in ways other than those outlined above. To cite one example, while this may not be part of your responsibility, you should at least be aware of the need for responsible financial management in your organization. To cite the poster child for irresponsible financial management and actual criminal fraud activity, we need only remember the Enron scandal of 2001, in which key officials used a variety of accounting loopholes and actual misrepresentations to hide billions of dollars in company losses. People went to jail as a result of that scandal, and hundreds of employees lost the major portions of their retirement savings.

Since that time, legislation has been enacted (the Sarbannes-Oxley Act of 2002) whose intent is to ensure transparency in accounting practices and provision for responsible corporate management. Sarbannes-Oxley requires the certification of financial statements, codes of ethics, retention of financial records, so-called "fitness to serve" rules for corporate officers, and protections for whistleblowers—those who bring to light potentially illegal practices they observe in their organizations.

Enron, which recorded over 100 billion dollars in revenue in the year 2000, was destroyed through the irresponsible, criminal behavior of its highest corporate officers. Arthur Andersen, the global accounting firm that audited Enron, also went out of business.

The lesson for all of us from the Enron story and its aftermath is that we need to keep our financial and ethical houses in order. Learn the word "transparency" as it applies to the overall management of your organization. Sarbannes-Oxley, through its code of ethics rule, offers good advice to all organizations in that regard, recommending that they establish and observe a strict code of ethics that applies to all areas of operation.

Theft

Anything in an organization can be stolen: money, physical assets, proprietary company information, identities, life, health and reputation. We discussed how personal life, health and company assets can be affected by violence in the workplace and natural disasters in the early part of this chapter, but the lifeblood of an organization can be lost through these other kinds of "thievery" as well.

As a manager in your organization, do a walkthrough of the facility in which you work and ask yourself how secure it is, and how secure the people and assets inside it are. For example, as we asked earlier, are emergency exits identified clearly? Is adequate lighting in place both inside and outside the building? Are doors locked (especially those at the rear of the building)? Are valuables locked away securely—those belonging to both individuals and the company? Is a security system installed (one that people understand and can access quickly)?

And while it may not be "theft" as we customarily think of it, what about the security of your organization's computer systems? Is your electronic information secure from viruses? Is information pass code protected? Do you have rules and policies governing the use of company owned computers and software? About the use of a company intranet and the internet? Irresponsible and deliberately criminal use of IT assets can do severe damage to organizations. You need to be aware of your "interface" with these systems and those who use them, and do your part to prevent loss and disruption of company activity.

Knowledge Transfer and Succession Planning

An interesting thing happens in manufacturing facilities, especially those that have been in operation for a long time. I used to see this frequently in paper mills for example. Over time, countless upgrades and modifications occur to equipment and control systems. Pipes are rerouted, new control panels installed, and new interlocks put in place (connections that link one phase of an operation to another— for example, a controller that activates a pump when liquid in a tank reaches a certain level). What will happen over time is that only "Old Bill," who has worked in maintenance for the past 40 years, knows how a given part of the operation works. And the problem is, often the information is recorded in Old Bill's neural pathways—his brain—and nowhere else.

The kind of information locked away in Bill's head is invaluable, and you need to get it out of there. You need to commission someone to work with Bill to extract that information, and get your systems carefully documented, both with actual engineering drawings and diagrams, and with related training materials for employees.

Bill, in other words, is an invaluable knowledge resource. His knowledge is a competitive asset that his organization can't afford to lose. For any organization, the basics of knowledge management and knowledge transfer are pretty simple: an organization needs to know where its critical information resides; what formats it's in; who has access to it; what can be done when necessary to reproduce and share it; and what processes are in place to preserve it. Ask these questions of your organization. Losing key company information constitutes a serious risk to the organization's current and future well being. In many cases it's your competitive advantage.

A similar point can be made in regard to succession planning. This can apply to Bill. Who is going to replace him? How will this individual acquire Bill's knowledge, skill and ability? If the answers to these questions are "I don't know," then you need to discover some answers, sooner rather than later.

This applies to any key member of an organization. In small companies especially, often virtually all expertise resides in the person of a key contributor—often the owner/operator of the business. The risks inherent in this situation are many. The first is business continuation. What happens if this individual becomes disabled or dies? Plans need to be in place for the ongoing operation of the business, and financial instruments (e.g. insurance policies) need to be in place to secure assets.

On a somewhat smaller scale, think about any key contributor in your organization—say, for example, a sales manager. What do you do if you lose that individual? What kind of "bench strength" do you have, in regard to a replacement? Succession plans are those that identify key contributors, and set up training/mentoring plans to prepare successors to those individuals. To return to a sports analogy, does a football team at any level have only one quarterback? Absolutely not. When the starter goes down, someone needs to be prepared and ready to take the next snap from the center. Not having people in your organization prepared and ready to assume a greater level of responsibility is another area of risk you can't afford to ignore.

Wake up.

I said that those words would comprise my basic message in this chapter. Of course I could only touch on several of the kinds of risks that can strike any of our organizations. Hopefully we reviewed enough of these to get your attention.

Unexpected things can and do happen all the time in organizations, and to sleepily ignore this fact is to invite even more serious consequences when they do happen. The best defense against the unforeseen is to foresee it, to make responsible preparations for it. You owe this kind of preparation to yourself and to the people around you.

Wake up; wake your people up.

Fur Further Consideration

1. From your experience, describe a risk that actually "came to life" in an organization you were a part of. What preparation had been made for it? What were the effects of the experience? Did the organization take steps to alleviate that category of risk for the future? What were these steps?
2. In your current working life, which categories of risk do you see as the most serious? Why?
3. For the risk category just mentioned, what is the organization doing to alleviate it? Do you see these actions as adequate? Why or why not?
4. Have you ever been the first one to arrive at the scene of an accident, or to respond to the aftermath of criminal activity of some kind? What did you do? Considering what you did, would you change anything should a similar situation present itself? What would you do differently?
5. Where does valuable information reside in your organization? How is that information managed?—that is, how is it stored, preserved, reproduced and accessed? In your mind, are the processes in place for accomplishing

the foregoing adequate? If you could change any of these processes, what changes would you make?

6. Does your organization do succession planning? What is your assessment of this process? Is it fair? Is it adequate? If any, what changes would you suggest?

7. How is IT managed in your organization? In your opinion, are these assets adequately protected from risk? How could existing protections be strengthened?

8. The point is made early in this chapter that we no longer live in Kansas. While horrific events such as the shooting in Huntington Beach seem to happen all too frequently, is it possible for us to over-emphasize this kind of risk? How do we keep from scaring people unnecessarily in our current culture, while at the same time taking all responsible efforts to assess and manage risk?

16 DISCIPLINE AND ACCOUNTABILITY

Discipline

Think for a moment about how you use the word "discipline" or "disciplined." We often use the term in its negative sense. We say our neighbors' children lack discipline; they're always climbing the fence and raiding our rutabaga patch. We say that a given army is an undisciplined rabble. Of ourselves, we say we lack the discipline needed to lose fifteen pounds.

A possible common denominator in these instances is that those involved appear to lack the inner resolve needed to conduct themselves in a more desirable way. If the neighbor kids had this resolve they'd realize the error of their ways and stay in their own yard. The army would wear starched uniforms and march in straight lines. We'd change our eating habits and lose the fifteen pounds.

"Discipline" can refer to an inner resolve, a strong, core sense of what the correct course of action is in a given situation. It can be thought of as the *will* needed to act in a given way. The will needed may come from an even deeper core of values, a core not readily shaken by competing demands or varying conditions.

Two additional factors that affect discipline are recognition and acceptance. The neighbor kids need to perceive, then recognize that their behavior is not what it needs to be. There also has to be a kind of switch inside them that, when activated, accepts what they've perceived. The final component is the resolve or discipline just described—the power to act and actually do something different.

A related definition of the word "discipline" refers to the behaviors we engage in when we try to bring about a "correct," more desirable course of action. We discipline our dogs when they urinate on the rug. We remove our children's hands when they reach toward the top of a hot stove. We take away casual dress on Fridays when our employees report to work wearing tank tops, shorts and flip flops.

The second key term in this chapter's title is "accountability." When we declare ourselves accountable for something, we assume responsibility for it. I'm accountable each month, for example, for making sure that the house payment gets made on time. I'm prepared to say that there can't be accountability without discipline. We can't guarantee results in the workplace, for example, until people exercise the discipline needed to do what we assign them to do, and until they "own" their tasks and assume responsibility for them.

Recognition and acceptance affect responsibility in the same way they do discipline. In my house payment example, I need to perceive the need for paying the mortgage versus using that money for the trip to Bermuda. I need to recognize that paying the mortgage is a more desirable behavior than taking the money to the casino. In my heart I need to *accept* this as the best thing for me to do.

We want our people to exercise discipline and accountability as they go about their tasks. The question of the hour, and for this chapter is, how do we make that happen?

Consequences

When I was still an undergraduate doing my student teaching in a large Seattle-area high school, I asked my cooperating teacher what the "main thing" was in dealing with high school classes. He said, "If you threaten to knock a student under the table if he does something, and then he does that something, you have to knock him under the table." Let me hasten to add that he was not advocating violence; he was making the point that if you said you were going to do something, you had to do it.

The general meaning I derive from this is that others will do what we ask if they're certain that a given consequence will occur if they don't. Again, in a figurative sense, they don't want to get knocked under the table. After being stopped twice for speeding on a certain road in the State of Mississippi, I learned not to speed there. I knew what would happen if I did, and I didn't want that to happen again.

Of course we can look at this in a positive way as well. We act in certain ways because we want to have a good opinion of ourselves, and we want others to share that opinion. We've all had bosses, for example, whom we wanted to please, and for whom we'd run through a wall. Some athletic coaches can instill this discipline in their players in various ways. They instill in their players a will to perform that perhaps the players themselves wouldn't be able to generate. To quite a degree, this is what we strive to do as managers.

Apparently we do what we do in every arena in life because of consequences. Aubrey Daniels is one who has articulated this idea repeatedly and persuasively in a number of books. He calls his psychology of behavior ABC, which stands for Antecedent, Behavior, Consequence[1].

Antecedents are what we engage in to try and elicit a given behavior. We order our children to clean their rooms. We threaten dire consequences if they don't. The rooms remain in their deplorable condition, but we back off of our threats. We try other tactics, offering rewards if the rooms get cleaned. Everything we do in order to bring about the behavior is an antecedent in the sense that it happens before the desired behavior (the cleaning of the room). When a given antecedent doesn't work, we're often tempted to repeat it, as Daniels phrases it, in a louder, longer and meaner way. Thus the behavior of some parents we observe in the supermarket, threatening ominous consequences if their children don't vacate the toy aisle immediately.

Daniels defines antecedents in a very broad way. In his view anything that comes before behavior is an antecedent acting to influence it. In this expanded view, organizational culture itself is always functioning as an antecedent, telling us in both direct and indirect ways what is acceptable and what isn't. This is why it's extraordinarily difficult to change a culture and behavior that has become customary within that culture.

Understand that I never watch this show, but the TV show "Wife Swap" illustrates this point well. The show takes a wife from one very distinct culture (characterized for example by strict rules), and drops her into another distinct culture, often a very permissive one. The same thing happens to the wife who has been living in a more permissive culture. All her antecedents shape her to behave in the ways approved of in her more relaxed home environment, so she too experiences culture shock when she's dropped into a more strict family environment.

We see this phenomenon in organizations when they reach a tipping point and decide that they must be run by policies, instead of by much more informal understandings of what individual managers want. When this occurs, all of employees' antecedents have been those of the earlier, tribe-like culture; it can be a shock to them to experience the new antecedents, the ones requiring them to learn rules and policies—and to experience consequences if they don't abide by them.

So understand that antecedents emerge from the entire culture, but focus now on a specific kind of antecedent, the actual directions we give our people as to what we want them to do.

As managers, Daniels says we emphasize antecedents, all the things we do to bring about an action or behavior on the part of someone. You for example say to a subordinate, "I need you to re-check tomorrow's shipping schedule and make sure it's right before you leave for the day." That's the **antecedent**. What the subordinate does in response is the **behavior**, and the **consequence** is what happens if he does or doesn't do what you ask.

Performance Management

Let me repeat that last clause: The consequence is what happens if he does or doesn't do what you ask. If, from his experience with you, he knows that there will be no meaningful consequence one way or the other, then whether or not the behavior you ask for occurs or not is pretty much left to chance. This is also why the child remains in the toy aisle. From prior experience, he knows his parent's threats, no matter how shrill, will lead to nothing unpleasant.

Let me re-emphasize my point about antecedents. Those are easy, which is part of the reason why we gravitate toward them. We will cite chapter and verse about what we want someone to do; we will go to elaborate lengths, even showing him/her pictures and diagrams of what we want things to look like—and then we're surprised when our efforts don't yield the results we're after. Daniels provides a compelling example of an ineffective antecedent, the warnings on cigarette packages. He asks if we've ever seen a smoker look at a pack of cigarettes, read the warning, then say, "Whoa! I better not smoke these babies!" And of course we never see that.

Our smoker is going to light up, because he knows what the consequences will be. In Daniels' terminology, he knows that the consequences of his action are going to be Positive, Immediate and Certain (this is a PIC consequence in Daniels' terminology). The smoker will like the feeling of relief as he inhales (this is the Positive part); he will get that feeling right away (this is the Immediate part); and he knows this will happen because of much prior experience (this is the Certain part).

By contrast, what will happen if our worker fails to check the shipping schedule? It all depends. In many cases, nothing of any consequence will happen. Perhaps you'll give him a disapproving look; perhaps you'll ask him why he didn't check the schedule; perhaps you'll say something like, "Don't let this happen again!" None of these consequences will be necessarily pleasant, but they are unlikely to deter our worker from ignoring future directions. These consequences are simply not strong enough to shape future behavior. Like the people in the "Wife Swap" families, he'll continue to be reinforced by the prevailing culture he's been a part of.

Potential consequences are either positive or negative depending on the employee's perception of them. In the case of our worker, if his life basically proceeds unchanged (he's none the worse for wear, so to speak), then your reactions will be perceived as positive. The culture is sustained. Any future consequence is apparently perceived as future versus immediate (as in the immediate nicotine rush the smoker experiences), and as to its certainty, nothing in his experience tells him that the possible "bad thing" will happen at all. So, why take your request to check the shipping schedule seriously?

As I say, we managers tend to be good as givers of antecedents; we are less good as arrangers of meaningful consequences. Daniels says that our efforts as managers may be as high as 85% as givers of antecedents, versus 15% as arrangers of consequences. He says that the balance should be more like 50/50.

Where does this reluctance come from—to arrange meaningful consequences? It can come from ignorance; we simply don't know we're supposed to do it. It can come from fear; we're afraid that people will think less of us if we "come down on them." Related to this, it can come from a misplaced desire to be "one of the guys/girls." You've learned that when you step into manager shoes, being "one of the gang" is no longer possible. Our reluctance to arrange consequences can also come from the kind of personality we have. Many of us simply don't welcome what we see as confrontation; as calling people on behavior that they need to change.

If we're to get the results we want in the workplace, the people who work for us need to carry out their duties and responsibilities. A blessed thing occurs when they develop the core that I referred to earlier—the will to engage with their tasks and carry them out to positive conclusions. Sometimes they develop this disciplined approach on their own; other times it has to come from the way we manage them, including the way we arrange appropriate consequences. This sometimes must occur as part of a seismic shift in the culture, such as the one mentioned earlier, when an organization goes from what could be called management by personality to management by policy.

Positive Discipline

The most uncomfortable role supervisors and managers play is that of disciplinarian, the one who metes out punishment when people break rules or fail to meet work standards. Even so-called progressive discipline is a pain in the backside, and we avoid it if we possibly can—affecting both current performance and workforce morale in a bad way. Progressive discipline is the practice of moving from verbal warning to first written warning to final written warning to suspension to termination. To all that let me say, "Blech." The problem with this process is that the manager/supervisor is the one who assumes responsibility for an employee's performance, and that is exactly backwards. If you are doing this, stop it.

My life in this arena was changed when I read a book called *Discipline Without Punishment* by Dick Grote[2]. This book is literally transformative. What Grote does is turn the supervisor from overseer to guide and helper. It begins by clarifying expectations, and asking an employee directly if she understands what the expectations are. You say something like, "You do understand that the responsibility to meet these expectations is yours, don't you?" As soon as the employee responds "Yes I do," the dye is cast, your future role as guide and helper versus whip cracker is established.

Here is what can happen as the employee embarks on her job with you. Let's say at some future point she begins to miss work or starts arriving late. Initially, you call this to her attention in an informal way, but it does become a problem. You ask to talk to her and remind her of your earlier conversation—about your expectations and requirements. Perhaps you say, "Do you remember when we talked earlier? Do you remember when you said you understood that the responsibility for meeting these expectations was yours?"

Of course she agrees. Then you say, "What else can I do to help you address this?" The two of you brainstorm ways that she can solve her attendance problem (a new alarm clock? a bus instead of an unreliable car?) She thanks you profusely, you document the meeting, and that's that.

But a fly emerges in the ointment. A couple of weeks later she's late. A day later, she calls in saying that she has to take a child to the doctor. You need to talk to her again. At this meeting, once again, you communicate the seriousness of the situation, but perhaps add, "What else can we think of that will help you resolve this?" More brainstorming occurs; more reminders given of what might happen if she's unable to get to work often and on time.

Subsequent meetings may occur if she doesn't improve. Throughout, the employee is endlessly grateful for what you're trying to do. A final step is sometimes a Decision

Making Day, with pay, during which your employee talks with her family, then drafts a letter detailing last commitments she's willing to make. If she doesn't return with the letter, her employment ends and is classified as a voluntary quit. What you have in this instance is a "no fault divorce." You say to yourself "We're a good company, she's a good person, but we just couldn't make this work."

Supervisors, often with moist eyes, would tell me that our initiating the "positive discipline" program was the most significant thing that ever happened in their working lives. Get the book; read it immediately; throw out your existing program and implement this one.

Ensuring Accountability

Accountability thus begins with employees realizing who is responsible for effective performance. They are. The consequences for sub-par performance are best administered in a positive discipline approach like the one described above. Remember, however, that this isn't a passive process; it is a purposeful, intentional one. It is one that you stay on top of. You are the one who must make clear tasks, rules and performance standards (e.g. for production and quality), and take action when necessary. You don't get to watch from the sidelines.

Let's turn our attention back to you. If you are to be successful as a manager, you need to deal in an intentional way with this concept of accountability. The most well conceived, carefully thought-out programs for ensuring operational success won't succeed unless managers assume accountability for them (unless managers come to own them). If there are to be failures or simply substandard performance, those will appear under your name.

You will only be as successful as the people who work for you, and unless you make *them* truly accountable, you won't achieve the results you're seeking.

What I've seen numerous times in my career is a reluctance on the part of managers at all levels to assume this accountability. They won't identify the consequences and follow through on them. Again, we tend to be okay with the antecedent part, of saying "This is what you have to do," but we are too often reluctant to take the next step—to follow through with the appropriate consequence when the employee doesn't meet the required standard. In this way, we get in the workplace the performance that we deserve from our people. We preserve the prevailing culture, one in which long-standing behaviors are allowed to continue.

Depersonalizing Accountability

I describe above how much I like the positive discipline program articulated by Dick Grote. One thing that program does is significant in a larger way. When we have a process such as positive discipline, it takes attention and pressure away from us as individuals, and places the attention where it belongs—on the process. It's the same with any set of rules or policies. In their absence, everything falls on you to interpret and enforce, and you're thrown back on your own experience, preferences, attitudes and perhaps prejudices to identify an appropriate course of action. In time, this will burn you out. It will also lead to a chaotic workplace if your fellow managers and supervisors are doing the same thing.

Once employees come to understand the processes, and once they have a chance to see that you will abide by rules and policies as they're written, you will be a long way toward getting the results you seek from them. They will want to see consistency, but that isn't so difficult to provide. The moment, however, that you let something slide, they will pick up on that. That will become an antecedent affecting future behavior. It will say to them, "My own observance of this rule can slide, because Juanita flagrantly disobeyed the rule and nothing happened to her." The consequence will be lessened accountability for performing to required standards. Don't let that happen.

Having advocated an emphasis on process, I do have to say a word here about personality. The way you go about managing to a policy or a process matters. Who you are as a person matters. The character you display day in and day out matters. Whether your people like and respect you or not matters. I think employees liking us without respecting us is not so good; it's better when those two go together.

This is, in the end, a practical matter, even a matter of productivity. You want your employees concentrating on the jobs they have to do. You don't want them worrying about you. They don't want you to be moody. They want to be able to count on you, to know that the things you stand for today you'll stand for tomorrow. They need you to be a fellow human being, someone who's going to "have their back," someone who's trying to clear the deck and make the operation run more smoothly. Someone who'll remove difficulties instead of *being* a difficulty.

Rather than think about the authority you possess due to your position, a thing to think about is the power you have. Authority is assigned; power is earned. You know of people who have no prescribed authority, but who have great power to influence people and events. Power can be exerted from anywhere in an organization. It's good if it can come from us as managers and supervisors, directed toward the important goals of our departments and organizations.

Remember too a point made earlier in the book, that we are the removers of obstacles, the sharpeners of machetes, often the teachers of proper machete technique, the suppliers of breaks and cool water. We exist to facilitate the work of others. Let me say that another way. We exist to facilitate the work of others.

Clarifying the Vision

The two concepts described in this chapter are enormously important, perhaps more than any others that we've dealt with. We want our people to be disciplined, exercising the strength of will needed to carry them (and us!) through the most trying of circumstances. We want them to be accountable, owning those circumstances. I understand that in the end these qualities always need to germinate and then express themselves from a place deep inside each of us as individuals.

When Covey[3] talks about this he suggests that our first "answer" as to why people fail to generate these qualities is that they lack determination or motivation—the "will power" needed to carry them through. He says that's not true. What he says is that they fail to truly engage and perform at high levels because deep inside they lack commitment to some larger vision or purpose. In his mind that is the fuel needed to sustain movement toward the goals we have for them.

If he's right, this points us as managers in a clear direction. What we need to do is discover, clarify and describe for them the larger vision we have for them and for everyone who's part of the organization. Jesus of Nazareth did this when He spoke of the Kingdom of God. Dr. King articulated it when he said "I have a dream."

I know. I put us in some lofty company there, but I hope you see the point. "Discipline," remember, comes from the word "disciple." People will follow us, showing great discipline and assuming accountability, only to the degree that they understand and accept both the path and the destination we've put before them.

As we think about our paths and destinations, we need to remember again that success on our respective journeys is not about us, but about those (our people) who are traveling with us. If you are a football fan of some years, you may recall how Alabama's legendary coach Bear Bryant viewed himself and his teams. Whenever there was a loss (very rare), the responsibility was his. Whenever there was a win, all the credit went to the players and the assistant coaches.

Coach Bryant was practicing what experts years later were to identify as a key attribute of successful managers and leaders. That attribute, perhaps somewhat surprisingly, is humility. It's obvious when you think about it; the more we're able to recognize and elicit the value of others, the more that value expands, and because of that expansion, the easier the path ahead will be.

Remember too that who we are as people does matter. The destinations we envision for our people will have meaning, in part, to the degree we show ourselves worthy of them. As we proceed along the paths we've laid out, we have to keep walking the talk that first set all of us in motion.

I loved it, for example, when Coach Bryant would talk about the next Saturday's opponent. Even when the opponent was the Little Sisters of the Valley, Coach Bryant would say, "Well, we're going to prepare, we're going to show up and do the best we can." All respect, all credit to the other side. No self-aggrandizement, certainly no chest-beating.

Little wonder that those Alabama teams proceeded so successfully in the direction of their dreams.

For Further Consideration

1. What is an area in your personal or working life in which you see discipline operating effectively? What factors can you identify that apparently facilitate this effectiveness?

2. In organizations you've worked in, have you seen a reluctance on the part of managers and supervisors to hold workers accountable? In addition to the suggestions in the chapter as to why this might be the case, what else do you think can cause this reluctance? Can you suggest ways to overcome it?

3. This chapter contains an explanation of Aubrey Daniels' ABC model of performance. Can you say how this model works in your own words? Give an example in which the consequence of a given behavior was not in line with the antecedent that preceded the behavior. Why do you think the inappropriate, or unlooked for consequence occurred?

4. Have you ever been involved in "writing up" an employee who broke a rule or whose performance wasn't measuring up? How did that experience go? Looking back on it, can you think of ways that you could have changed the outcome, or made the process of the write up in general more successful?

5. What is your assessment of the "accountability factor" in general? Do you think most organizations do a good job of ensuring accountability? If they ever miss the mark, why do you think they do? What could they do to improve in this area?

6. Can good managers be bad people? Can good people be bad managers? Explain your answers.
7. Are you surprised that humility is seen as a key quality for managers to aspire to? Do you think our culture as a whole values humility? How much of a "sell" do you think it would be to convince managers and supervisors that humility is something they should cultivate? How do you tell people that true humility always comes from a position of strength versus one of weakness?

Notes

1. Daniels, Aubrey C., Ph.D. *PERFORMANCE MANAGEMENT: Improving Quality Productivity Through Positive Reinforcement*. Tucker, Georgia: Performance Management Publications, 1989. Print.
2. Grote, Dick. *Discipline Without Punishment*. New York: AMACOM, 2006. Print.
3. Covey, Stephen. *The 7 Habits of Highly Effective People*. New York: Free Press, 2004. Print.

17 SERVICE

A Service Orientation

I remember being struck by a particular passage in Christian Scripture some years ago. This is from the 20th Chapter of Matthew: ". . .whoever desires to become great among you, let him be your servant. And whoever desires to be first among you, let him be your slave—just as the Son of Man did not come to be served, but to serve, and to give His life a ransom for many."

This is a startling statement, this idea that the Messiah didn't come to be served, but to serve. As with many other values and principles that have come down to us from the Judeo-Christian tradition (take care of the widows, feed the hungry), this one has some resonance and staying power. I think it's a good idea.

In previous chapters we've talked about you as a manager, about how you perceive yourself in the many different dimensions of your job. We've talked about how you need to realize that all of those dimensions are there, and that you need to "express" or embody each of them as occasions require: you have to attend to your people; you need to manage money and other resources; you need to be courageous in the face of technology; you need to be ready should an emergency arise; and so on. You step into and out of these dimensions as you work to keep all those beans moving across the field.

Service, to me, is not so much a dimension as it is an orientation. It colors all of the other dimensions. More than any other aspect of your job, service is a mindset; it's part of the frame of reference through which you view and interact with the world. I've suggested characteristics of this mindset in prior chapters. In our last chapter, for example, I said that you are the sharpener of machetes, the teacher of proper machete techniques, the supplier of breaks and cool water. This description skates close to the "servant" profile that Jesus spoke of.

I promise I'm not trying to convert you in the paragraphs that follow. I just want you to consider what it means to view yourself as someone who believes he/she is here to be served, versus someone who believes he/she is here to serve. The side of this equation we land on has serious implications for our lives generally, and for our lives as managers specifically.

Service as a Practical Matter

How do we usually define "service"? We have, to consider one application, Customer Service Departments in businesses and organizations. Those departments assist customers with issues and questions the customers have about products and services. In order to provide answers, customer service representatives need to know a great deal about the offerings of their organizations (one helped me the other day, for example, with questions about the router we use in our wireless system).

Even when it isn't being provided by a dedicated department, service is delivered any time there is an interaction or transaction between people for any purpose. The person bagging my groceries is delivering a service; the people who send the utility bill are providing a service; the person who cuts the little remaining hair I have is delivering a service.

In manufacturing facilities, departments "upstream" deliver services to those "downstream." In corrugated plants, for example, paperboard must be corrugated before it can be printed and slotted; printed before it can be "joined" (one end of a box-to-be needs to be glued, stapled or stitched to the other); joined before it can be bundled or banded; and so on. The downstream functions are customers receiving service from upstream providers.

Perhaps especially in the context of a dedicated customer service department, service can be seen almost as a commodity; it's an entity that must be delivered in an effective way if transactions of whatever kind or duration are to be conducted satisfactorily and repeated in the future. This applies outside dedicated customer service departments as well. Caremart, you recall, has lost all Hall family jewelry business due to the poor customer service delivered by Sales Associate Sarah.

Service is enabling. It's the commodity that greases the skids of all successful transactions that occur within human organizations and between individual human beings. It is that which cements or eventually breaks apart relationships—customer relationships and any other kind.

Service in Relationships

If you've worked in an organization containing human beings, you have probably realized that we don't quite have this service thing down yet. Especially in large organizations, you see what has been called the "silo effect," characterized by departments effectively walling themselves off from one another. Rummler and Brache, whom we've met earlier, talk about this, and their thoughts about it are reflected in the title of their book—*Managing the White Space on the Organization Chart* [1]. The white space is the space between the siloes. It's the place where skids need to be greased and relationships nurtured. Departments need to work with one another, not against one another. As a manager, you need to play a key role in ensuring that this happens.

As members of departments, we appear to extend to our departments attitudes and feelings that we have for ourselves as individuals. It's hard for many of us to move out of a "me first" orientation. Stephen Covey would say of this that we may need to move along the "Maturity Continuum," which he sees as extending from Dependence (me first) to Independence (I can do this myself) to Interdependence (we can do this together). Understanding and embodying the qualities of interdependence is key if we are to develop a meaningful service orientation. We are not in our departments (or stores or repair shops or marriages) to be served, but to serve.

In trying to serve others, we first need to acknowledge and then control our egos. Ego is our sense of ourselves, our understanding of the unique collection of attributes that sets us apart from others. It's also our assessment of and feelings about those attributes. It's okay if we have positive feelings about who we are and what we do—it's even necessary that we have these feelings. Accomplishment (the achievement of purpose) can't spring from nothing; it has to spring from knowledge, competence and skill that are the products of a healthy ego. There's also the matter of will power. Will, that which drives accomplishment, also has a strong ego component at its base.

Ego "informs" all relationships. Strong, interdependent relationships have to be at least two-sided, and they can't be if one party either, a) Needs to impose ego demands on the other, or, b) Requires constant feeding of his/her fragile ego by the other party(s). Thus we don't want to extinguish ego. We need a strong sense of who we are and what we can do.

The difficulty has to do with our purposes for developing this sense of who we are, and for becoming ever more knowledgeable about what we might be able to accomplish. If we use a strong sense of our own capabilities for the good of others (and the institutions that these others inhabit), then I think we're fine. It's when we develop our egos *for their own sake* that we can run into trouble, feeling that we as individuals are somehow owed homage by the rest of the planet. This is what the phrase "ego maniac" means; it refers to one who's lost the ability to use the "Off" button that feeds his/her ego. A service orientation is going to require that we become self*less* versus self*ish*.

Jim Collins (*Good to Great*)[2] has this idea in mind when he makes his "not where but who" point. That point is simply that the "bus" (the organization) won't arrive where it needs to go if the wrong people are on board, or if the right people are in the wrong seats. My point is that rarely are the right people those with over-developed egos, those whose participation in any endeavor is always about what they can get out if for themselves, versus what the organization as a whole can accomplish. Remember the title of *this* book: *Managing on Purpose*. Rarely is the achievement of organizational purpose about you, except as your activity facilitates the forward movement of the entire enterprise.

The forward movement of the enterprise is often the result of successful relationships. These aren't possible without a service orientation. Here's a fact; it has to do with something that each of us is really good at. What each of us is really good at is being critical of ourselves; in this regard, as the old saying goes, we are our own worst enemies. My question for you is, since we are already so good at this *ourselves*, why do we participate in relationships with others who seek to do this (make us feel bad) *for* us?—seek to make us feel worse about who we are and what we're doing?

As social beings, we need the company of others. But in relationship to others individually or severally, shouldn't the core purpose of the relationship be the nurturing and strengthening of the people involved in it? Especially in an organization founded for a specific purpose (and they all are), isn't our role to build up the collective body of people, so that they *all* help the organization move forward?

In light of this, why would a Safety Manager seek to undermine a Production Manager? A Quality Manager seek to undermine an HR Manager? Everyone seek to undermine the General Manager? All of these pilgrims should build one another up, the better to keep the bus running strongly and pointed in the right direction.

You as a manager need to take this to heart. You need to pay attention to every relationship you have in the workplace; your first thought in every encounter with any of these people is "What can I do for you?" Or better yet, given the emphasis in this chapter, "How can I serve you?" Every transaction you have with another during the day should be a productive one. Every transaction should leave the other party or parties feeling if not actually good, at least that the encounter with you was a step in a positive direction.

Not every transaction you have is going to be a pleasant one, understand, because a given transaction may involve someone whose personal agenda may not be matching up exactly with that of the organization. As a manager, yours always does. Your purpose, your reason for being, is to move the organization forward. You don't need to keep having unpleasant transactions with people. Not to be harsh or unfeeling here, but not everyone belongs on the bus. You may need to be the one to help someone find another seat, or perhaps find another bus.

Yourself as Input

Chapter Five. The chapter in which we talked about filters and screens. Not everything gets through. You need to control inputs that come at you, expanding some, changing mesh size on other screens, making sure you have a "divert" screen. Assigning the highest priorities to the largest diameter screens. Watching the dashboard in that cockpit to make sure that nothing of importance is being ignored.

Here's my question for you here in *this* chapter. Among all the inputs coming at you, where are you? Yes, that's what I asked: where are *you*? I ask this because, as reluctant as I am to suggest this, I think you are a key input that comes at you every day. You have to manage that input at least as attentively and carefully as you do any other. In short, you need to manage yourself.

Aha! There you are! Trying to crawl out of the pipe! Well, it's not going to work! We both know you're in there!

Here's what I mean by each of us being in the pipe, by each of us comprising a "dimension" that we need to acknowledge and manage.

When we arrive at work each day, we don't, in a sense, come alone. We bring with us the sum total of all our prior experience, along with thoughts and feelings that have accumulated about that experience. Call this "baggage" if you will; we all have it. To the extent that we can, we need to leave that baggage home; better yet, we probably need to rid ourselves of it altogether.

The baggage that we bring with us to the workplace each day has the power to shape our responses to all the other inputs that we have to deal with. What if, for example, we truly are inhibited by technology? How will that affect our responses to any technology-related input that lands in our lap? A new control system, for example, that we need to learn and use? Related to our lives on the planet, what if we are convinced that the end days are upon us, and that a catastrophe related to those is absolutely imminent—as in, it's arriving today? What if we're convinced that we'll never be able to relate to the Hispanic (or Caucasian or South Asian) employees who work for us? What will all these thoughts do to the way we set up our screens in our respective filters?

You see, I hope, that these kinds of thoughts could wreak havoc with our filters—with our input processing systems. Some inputs will be wildly out of proportion, some will be minimized to the point of invisibility—so small that they won't even sound an alarm on our dashboard. In short, what we bring into the control room with us is hugely important.

It's especially huge in light of this chapter, which is about our willingness and capacity to serve others. We serve others effectively only to the degree that we can get out of our own way. Only to the degree that we can lay our baggage down and see our instruments clearly. Only to the degree that we can set up our filters and screens to process inputs in the proportions that they need and deserve.

Look again at the sample filter from Chapter Five, reproduced for you on the next page.

When you can't get out of your own way, it's as if a large, murky screen envelopes all the other screens you see in the diagram. It has the power to distort and obscure all the other inputs that require our attention.

We've all known managers around whom we've had to tip toe. That's in part because of the baggage screen I just described. Such managers drag that screen into the workplace with them, and it keeps them from paying attention to other key dimensions of their jobs: you, the daily schedule, compliance—the list could go on. Inputs from these other dimensions don't have much of a chance of being processed.

If you have such a screen, you need to leave it at home. What can it possibly have to do with helping you achieve your organization's purposes? How can you develop the service orientation we describe in this chapter, if it is continually demanding to be served?

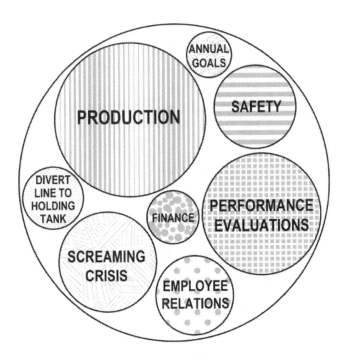

Service and the Culture

I understand that this serve versus being served orientation isn't exactly prevalent in our modern culture. Remember, however, the leadership quality that Jim Collins saw, that he referred to as Level 5 Leadership in his *Good to Great* companies; this is what I quoted back in Chapter Two: "Level 5 leaders channel their ego needs away from themselves and into the larger goal of being a great company. It's not that Level 5 leaders have no ego or self-interest. Indeed, they are incredibly ambitious—*but their ambition is first and foremost for the institution, not themselves."* So there is currency and support for the "servant leader" concept as it applies today.

We exist really as "vessels," conduits through which service can flow to those who need it. To my point above, we can't be occupying those vessels ourselves. We need to empty them out, as it were, so that larger purposes can be served through us. The Apostle Paul makes this point in the second chapter of his letter to the Philippians: ". . .if I am poured out as a drink offering on the sacrifice and service of your faith, I am glad and rejoice with you all." (Philippians Chapter Two, Verse 17).

Paul had a pretty good handle on this service idea, on the fact that he, Paul, wasn't the point—that "he" just needed to get out of the way. He says in his letter to the Galatians (Chapter 2, Verse 20) that "I have been crucified with Christ; it is no longer I who live, but Christ lives in me." What I think "I" means in that passage is that all the ego-related foibles characteristic of the man Paul have been pretty well extinguished. At that point he may be as self*less* as anyone I'm familiar with. In the place of Paul the human being was the mission—purpose—of the church he did so much to establish.

None of us is going to reach that standard in service to our organizations—we are not, as it were, going to die for them. But to the degree that we can, for both spiritual and practical purposes, we need to serve; we need to get out of our own collective ways.

For Further Consideration

1. This chapter says that service is more an "orientation" than a "dimension." Express this idea in your own words.

2. The chapter says that service is a commodity. If you had to assign a value to it, in terms of its impact on organizational success, what would that value be?

3. How would you characterize the "service relationships" you have now? Do you think your "customers" perceive the importance you place on service? Why/why not?

4. Do divisions or departments in your organization have a servant mentality or orientation? If your answer is "no," in your opinion would it be beneficial to develop such an orientation? How could you help bring it about?

5. Many don't consider Type A, hard-driving business people as "servant leaders." Is this accurate? Can these people become servant leaders? What would it take to make them realize the value of this kind of leadership?

6. What comes to your mind when you hear the word "ego"? Do most people in your circle have the kind of ego control described in this chapter? In general, what keeps people from developing this kind of control?

7. Can you think of a time recently when you couldn't "get out of your own way? What "hot buttons" or triggers in you cause you to jump into your own way? Can you think of ways to keep this from happening?

8. Have you seen the "silo effect" up close and personal? What impact does this effect have on the organization in which you see it?

9. How well do you think any of us can "empty ourselves" out (extinguish ego needs) in the pursuit of larger goals? Do you have experience doing this, or have you seen others do it? In either case, how were individuals able to accomplish it?

Notes

1. Brache, Alan P., and Rummler, Geary A. *IMPROVING PERFORMANCE: How to Manage the White Space on the Organization Chart*. San Francisco: Jossey-Bass, 1990. Print.
2. Collins, Jim. *Good to Great*. New York: Collins, 2001. Print.

18 LEADING

<u>Inspiring</u>

If you're a student of the Civil War, you remember the suicidal charge that General Pickett's men made across the open field on the third day of the Battle of Gettysburg. They were to advance more than a mile across an open field, with Union artillery arrayed on each side and in front of them—not to mention the reinforced, dug-in infantry dead ahead. General Pickett's men were cut to ribbons, and those few who could returned in shock and disarray back across the field.

General Robert E. Lee, who had ordered the charge, went out to meet them, saying in great distress that things would be alright, that it was all his fault, that the failure was entirely his. Here's the remarkable thing. After being almost totally decimated, having seen their friends and fellow soldiers slaughtered by the Union guns, the remnants of General Pickett's division were ready to go back! Some wanted Lee to let them have another crack at breaking through the Union line.

Assuredly there were other reasons why the Confederate soldiers would have made a second charge. They were fighting more than the Battle of Gettysburg; they were fighting for their families, their states, for the way of life they knew in the South. They had a lot of skins in the game, so to speak.

But everything we read about Lee suggests that he himself had a powerful influence on his men. They would literally die for him—as thousands did at Gettysburg. This in the face of tactics he employed there that, almost from the beginning, appear to be rather misguided. Lee had a hold on his men. As Pickett's charge attests, they would do anything, give anything that he asked, to the point of giving their lives.

Well, as managers and leaders in our organizations, we won't be asking our people to replicate Pickett's charge. I think, however, that it's a good and relevant question to ask how Lee did it: how leaders past and present are able to inspire commitment and effort in their people. When we say that they "inspire" their people, we mean that they breathe life and purpose into them. How do they do that?

We've supplied some answers to this question in the preceding chapters. We've talked about a "new you" that can emerge through looking at the frame of reference you bring to the workplace; this was back in Chapter Seven. In Chapter Eight we discussed the need for you to know and understand your people, the need for you to "clear the decks" and make it easier for them to accomplish their day-to-day tasks. In Chapter Sixteen we discussed ways that you make discipline a growth-producing factor for your people. And in our last Chapter on service, we said that it would be best if you sought to serve, rather than be served. The hold that we can come to exert on our people should be stronger to the degree that we can express these dimensions of ourselves as managers.

When we talk about "pure" leadership, however, we need to look a bit deeper.

Leaders and Managers

We've talked earlier about the difference between management and leadership; you recall that managers are the machete sharpeners, and leaders are the ones in the tops of the trees shouting "Wrong jungle!" In other words, leaders are thought to be the ones who determine direction (and motivate people to move in desired directions), and managers are the ones who do the practical things needed to ensure that movement in the desired direction actually occurs.

This distinction between leaders and managers is not a pure one. As managers, that is, we do need to employ leadership attributes and skills. We need to understand qualities of leadership and use them, in addition to what may be the more practical tools of management per se such as scheduling, administration and machete sharpening. It also helps if we're fully versed in the "content" of our respective fields (e.g. banking, plumbing, IT).

Let's begin our exploration of leadership by talking first about the employee, about the recipient of our leadership and management efforts. What is he or she looking for in the workplace?—from us?

We need to begin by acknowledging that most work is hard. I want to do that by returning once again to the box plant, to that place where my old foreman Bernie Stopko walked the floor, and talk about another significant person I knew there.

The following occurred the first morning I worked in the corrugated box plant. I was sent to be a stacker on something called an Equalok Folder Gluer, a machine that could fold and glue up to 15,000 boxes an hour. I was at the end of a conveyor, and bundles of twenty Lucky Lager Beer boxes came down the conveyor at me. The corrugated board of these boxes was waxed, and the bundles were untied. I was to grab these bundles and put them on pallets, making sure there were no bad ones, and that the loads didn't tip over. I had to learn this elaborate "chimney stack," in which the slippery, untied bundles were interlocked, one tier on top of another, and "tie sheets" inserted between the tiers to keep the loads stable.

Like Pickett's men, I thought I was going to die. It was hot, the machine looked and sounded like it was going 100 miles an hour, I had no help, I didn't know how to grab nor stack the bundles, and let me repeat—I had no help. Not that it wasn't available. A man was walking around the machine, occasionally pulling a box out of a hopper, examining it (for quality purposes), then continuing his leisurely walks around the machine. I quickly developed this hatred for him.

I was to learn that our Equalok crew consisted of an operator, an assistant operator (this person fed the unfolded boxes into a hopper at the back end of the machine), those who tied bundles and banded loads, a dedicated forklift operator, and me, the stacker.

Forget for a moment about inspiration. I was interested in survival. After a very short time I was asking myself, "Can I do this?", and the answer seemed to be a resounding "No!" The bundles continued to hurtle toward me down the conveyor.

I'm serious about the question in the last paragraph—the "Can I do this?" question—because it represents the first issue we need to resolve for our people: forget about inspiration for a moment. We need to ensure that people perceive that they can do the work we assign to them. That first morning on the Equalok Folder Gluer, I didn't think I could do the work.

I needed practical help. I needed that guy who was walking around the machine to tell me what to do and how to do it, which he eventually did. He was the operator, and he gave me a break after two grueling hours. I saw a ray of hope. He did the very first thing that managers need to do, and that is he helped me see that the job was *possible*. I understand that he wasn't a salaried supervisor or manager, but he was performing a management function.

Here is a difference I will pose between managers and leaders. If we are to unlock the discretionary effort that people have the potential to give, we need to move them through a continuum of attitudes ranging from "possible" all the way to "meaningful." Perhaps all the way to "important" or "significant." Operators, leads, supervisors and managers can establish the first phase—showing workers that jobs are possible—leaders are those who need to make work meaningful. They need to establish in workers' minds, "What I'm doing here is valuable; it makes a difference."

There are interim steps on the progression from possible to meaningful. The entire continuum, which changed for me on the Equalok depending on the product we were running, could go from possible to endurable to frustrating to faintly satisfying to almost enjoyable to meaningful. I'm sure you could add finer gradations of feelings/attitudes to that continuum, but you see my point.

Here is a footnote to the Equalok story that is important to the final point I'll make in this chapter. Our operator's name was Bob Quigley. Bob was a quiet guy, a veteran of World War II. He rarely talked at all, and when he did it was never small talk. He was the best of the three Equalok operators by a wide margin, and we were all pleased when we were assigned to his crew.

Years into my tenure in the corrugated plant, a new folder gluer was installed. We were talking in the break room one morning about the new machine's complexities, about how fast it would run and so on. Of particular interest to us was how many people it would take to run it—sure that it would take quite a few. That morning Bob looked up from his lunchbox and said, "Me and Jim could run that by ourselves."

Given what he said that morning—thinking about how much that meant to me—he could have been right. We could have run the new machine, just the two of us. I would have gone to the wall, so to speak, to prove that Bob's high assessment of me was warranted. His high assessment of me added meaning to the work that I did.

Motivation

The work. We need to talk about the work, the people who perform it, and your relationship to both. I said a moment ago that leadership is that which helps workers (or soldiers) see their work as significant, as having meaning. Try that with someone who rides on the back of a residential garbage truck, and who makes just a shade over the minimum wage. Try that with someone at the back of that Equalok Folder Gluer, who sees no relief coming.

We can say that meaning is supplied through the pay that people receive. It's supplied through fear that, as low as the pay might be, it is still pay, and individual workers would be lost without it. It may be supplied through relationships that people develop with their co-workers, and maybe as well through advancement they can see coming—should they be able to acquire the needed knowledge and skill.

In terms of what you are to supply in the way of leadership, let me return to my idea that you need to clear the decks for people. This is a threshold responsibility that you have. Given that much work is hard in and of itself, the least management owes its people is an attempt to keep the *de*motivating factors in the workplace minimized. Clutter, for example, is a demotivator. Supplies not being available is a demotivator. Excessive heat and noise are demotivators. Tools that are worn out are extremely demotivating. Trucks upon which required maintenance hasn't been performed are demotivating. Your being a dipstick and yelling at people is demotivating. In other words, our people have enough of a fight on their hands just with their assigned tasks; they shouldn't have to fight the workplace itself. You fight that fight for them.

Beyond this threshold responsibility, we can look at distinct types or styles of leadership, each of which can affect in different ways the responses we get from our people. These are articulated in a work we cited earlier by Bruce J. Avolio and Bernard M. Bass in their book *Developing Potential Across a Full Range of Leadership.*[1] Avolio and Bass divide these types of leadership into "Transactional" and "Trans-formational." The former focus on ways that managers handle individual "moments" with their people, designed to bring about a specific response or behavior. The latter, as the name suggests, is about deeper, transformational change that leadership styles can bring about. Here are the different types, broken into the two basic classifications.

Transactional Leadership

Laissez-Faire Leadership. This can be described as "watching" job performance and hoping for the best. While classified as transactional leadership, laissez faire leadership is actually the avoidance or absence of leadership. It is the most inactive form of leadership and also the most ineffective; under laissez-faire leadership, nothing is transacted (because the laissez faire leader/manager basically doesn't *do* anything!).

Management By Exception. As a transactional leadership strategy, management by exception can be active or passive. In the active mode, you set up standards or work targets, then wait to see who fails to meet them—you actively monitor deviation from your standards. You watch for mistakes and errors in your people's assignments, then take corrective action. In the passive mode, you don't set up the standards in advance. You simply wait for mistakes and errors to occur, then take corrective action. Management by exception, especially in the passive mode, is sometimes called "Gotcha!" management.

Contingent Reward. With this method, the transactional leader assigns or gets agreement on what needs to be done, and promises rewards or actually delivers rewards in exchange for satisfactorily carrying out the assignment. Contingent reward is sometimes called "Let's Make a Deal" management. The mother promising her child a cookie if he comes out of the toy aisle in the department store is practicing contingent reward management.

Transformational Leadership

Individualized Consideration. Those who practice individualized consideration pride themselves in knowing their people. They pay special attention to each individual's need for achievement and growth by acting as coaches or mentors. They create new learning opportunities and work at maintaining a supportive climate. They recognize individual differences in terms of what people need and want from their work. They encourage two-way exchange in communication and practice a lot of "Management by Walking Around."

Intellectual Stimulation. As this kind of transformational leader, you stimulate your followers' efforts to be innovative and creative. You encourage your people to question assumptions, redefine problems and approach old situations in new ways. You encourage creativity. You don't criticize individual members' mistakes (you probably wouldn't say, "Hall, if you can't run this machine. . ."). You solicit new ideas and creative problem solutions from your people, whom you include in the process of addressing problems and finding solutions. Your people are encouraged to try new approaches, and their ideas are not criticized if they differ from yours.

Inspirational Motivation. Transformational leaders do what we described earlier: they behave in ways that motivate and *inspire* those around them by providing meaning and challenge in their followers' work. A result is that team spirit is aroused and enthusiasm and optimism are displayed. The inspirationally motivating leader gets followers involved in envisioning attractive future states. The leader clearly communicates expectations that followers want to meet, and demonstrates commitment to the shared vision.

Idealized Leadership. If you are this kind of transformational leader, you behave in ways that make you a role model for your followers. Such leaders are admired, respected, and trusted. Followers identify with these leaders and want to emulate them. Among the things the leader does to earn this credit is consider the needs of others over his or her own personal needs (you recall much of our chapter on service). The leader shares risks with followers and is consistent rather than arbitrary. He or she can be counted on to do the right thing, demonstrating high standards of ethical and moral conduct.

Avolio and Bass make the point that none of these types or styles of leadership is bad, nor can any one of them stand as the one we should strive to be all the time. We need to monitor and adapt, utilizing these styles of leadership as appropriate. More than styles, we need to become the leaders in each of these ways as situations dictate. And no, it isn't just taking one hat off and putting another one on. It is having these modes of leadership as competencies, as integral dimensions of who we are as people that emerge as we summon them, or naturally in response to a given set of circumstances. We may seem to be acting intuitively, in other words, but we are responding with intuition that has been educated, that has been prepared in advance.

Saying this reveals my answer to the ancient question: are leaders born, not made? I will allow that both contribute to the final result, but certainly we can be "made"; we can expand upon our God given attributes and become increasingly more effective as leaders.

Made Not Born?

I just gave you my answer to this question. You have been prepared to be a manager. Perhaps you studied management in school; perhaps you've simply been managing for years and have a good handle on it now. Maybe you've gone through one or more of the major management development programs such as Development Dimensions International's *Interaction Management*. Online programs: you could turn on your computer now and find dozens of ways to learn more about management and leadership, to earn degrees and achieve certifications—to fill in perceived gaps in your preparation. You can go to that seminar next Saturday to brush up on just one aspect of management—perhaps interpersonal communication. There is no dearth of information available, deliverable in dozens of different ways. If you want to learn more, you certainly can.

I say all this in the context of what I called the ancient question: can managers be "made," or do we need to be born into this role? Does the same apply to leaders?

Management and leadership are about behavior. They emerge through the things we do day in and day out with our people. It is the behavior that our people see in us that determines what they will do for us, both in quality and in quantity (i.e., how well they work and how much they produce).

So as we've been seeing, the question becomes, how do we create in ourselves the capacity for behaviors that people will follow? Those behaviors can certainly be identified and developed through the kinds of learning experiences identified above. We can be better listeners and better speakers. We can learn to be both more and less assertive. There may be behaviors that you've never "tried on" before as a manager, and if this is the case, you need to do that.

I remember, for example, the first training I did with corporate executives in sexual harassment prevention and response. An early question in that training was, how do you receive a complaint of sexual harassment from an employee? Think for a moment about how you would present that concept to a group of executives, and how you would make sure that they could produce the required behavior should a situation call for it.

The shortest answer is, you would make them engage in the required behavior. After presenting information and describing the behaviors we were looking for, I made them role play the desired behavior. I played the role of an employee coming to them to report instances of sexual harassment that my female superior had engaged in. Of course they'd never been in that situation before. If our expectation was that they'd be able to handle such a situation should it actually develop, we needed to see them do it. So, we did. They performed with varying degrees of success, as you might expect. But here's the thing: it's completely unrealistic to expect people to say and do things in an effective way that they've never done before! You have to let them practice and experiment, then try again. These experiences comprise rehearsals for the "real" experiences that will follow on the job.

My point here is that we can indeed, through the kind of training just described, learn new skills and behaviors. The more those are practiced, the more ingrained and natural they become, and you, in effect, can "remake" yourself in specific ways.

So an answer to the ancient question in this section is that we can indeed make ourselves into more effective managers and leaders. We can learn and demonstrate the behaviors that will influence people to follow us. We can hardwire those behaviors in.

Let me conclude with a word about character, about authenticity. Regardless of personality profiles and even the leadership styles we've just been looking at, to be successful leaders our people require certain non-negotiable things from us. As they are buffeted about in the workplace, they need to be able to count on certain things. They need to be able to count on you.

I mentioned in an earlier chapter that I learned an important lesson about teachers. Kids don't need glitz and fancy footwork. Kids need people who are honest, consistent and dependable. They need people they can bounce off of, and trust that those people won't break. In fact, there's the key word: trust. This is what your people need from you. Much is to be said for the fact that you'll be there every day; you'll be there on time, waiting for them; you'll be clear in your expectations and you'll be fair in the consequences you administer when the expectations aren't met. It will be clear that you're guided by a reliable inner compass; it will be clear that you aren't flying blind, that you're managing on purpose.

Doing these things and being this kind of person may not be everything when it comes to being a leader, but it's a lot. It certainly qualifies as an excellent start.

For Further Consideration

1. Who is a person in your life who embodies the qualities that General Lee did?—for whom people would deliver extraordinary levels of performance? How did this person elicit this kind of dedication and commitment?
2. Do you have your own distinctions between management and leadership that we may not have touched on in this chapter? What are they?
3. Have you ever been thrown into a given job without the proper amount of preparation? Describe that, and say how you could have been better prepared. In your opinion, does this practice persist today?—putting people into jobs and tasks before they're ready for them? Why do you think this keeps happening?
4. Is it realistic to think that leaders can make employees' jobs meaningful, even significant? Explain your answer.

5. In your role as a leader/manager, how successful are you at identifying and removing demotivating elements from the workplace? Can you see any demotivating behaviors in yourself that you could minimize? What are they?

6. How do you feel about the "born-not-made" question? Are those of us who may feel that we've been "made" into leaders any less real or authentic than those who are apparently born for the role? Explain your answer.

7. Have you been led by people who might have been personally appealing and charismatic, but ultimately not effective as leaders? If so, what caused them to be less effective? Do you perceive that they could have brought about changes in themselves that would have increased their effectiveness? What might they have done?

8. Have you used the leadership styles characterized as "transactional"? Which ones, and how successful were they?

9. Is trust between managers and their people as important as stated in this chapter? Can you think of instances in which trust was broken? Did people try to get it back? How difficult was that, and how successful were they?

Notes

1. Avolio, Bruce J., and Bass, Bernard M. *Developing Potential Across a Full Range of Leadership*. Mahwah, New Jersey: Lawrence Erlbaum Associates, Inc. 2002. Print.

AFTERWORD

The two most important ideas in this book may be, 1) That the job of managing must be seen whole; and, 2) managing must be purposeful.

The first idea is important because unless we achieve and retain a broad perspective of our jobs as managers, we will miss things. The potential costs of allowing that to happen are too high. We can't, for example, neglect the confidentiality of employee data; we can't ignore the basic laws and regulations that affect the workplace.

The second idea is important because we have diminishing quantities of resources with which to accomplish our objectives. These are human resources, time resources and financial resources, to name only three. We need to accomplish as much as we can with the resources available to us. Unless we are proactive and intentional in that effort, valuable resources will be wasted.

Of the management dimensions covered in the book, which are most critical? Where should you start?

If I were making plans using this book as a starting place, I think I'd make a checklist of the chapters in the Applications section of the book, then devise a rating scale for myself in terms of my performance in each of the topics covered in Chapters 7 – 18. It might look like this:

Point Values	Description
5	I already have this dimension down pat.
4	Most of the time I can handle this dimension reasonably well.
3	About half the time I think I function well in this dimension of the job.
2	I can function in this dimension, but it's really hard for me.
1	I need some dedicated help learning to manage in this dimension.

Then I might score myself using a chart like this one:

Chapter/Topic	Score	Comments/Improvement Plan
Chapter 7 Change		
Chapter 8 People		
Chapter 9 Finance		
Chapter 10 Planning		
Chapter 11 EEO		
Chapter 12 ADA/Other		

Laws		
Chapter 13 Privacy & Protections		
Chapter 14 Technology		
Chapter 15 Risk		
Chapter 16 Discipline & Accountability		
Chapter 17 Service		
Chapter 18 Leading		
Other		

If I were asked which dimensions of the manager's job are most critical, and/or that I see most inconsistently addressed, I would start with Discipline and Accountability.

Here are my reasons for saying that. Before you can improve your results, perhaps implementing a number of important changes, you need to establish a threshold of control. Regardless of what has happened to date, you need to establish an agenda for your people, one that includes both what they're supposed to do and how they're supposed to do it. Then you manage to that agenda. While we don't want to establish a Gulag mentality in the workplace, people need to know that we're purposeful. They need to know that you mean what you say, and that there will be consequences if they don't do what you tell them to do.

Concentrate on making each transaction you have with individuals and groups in the workplace successful. Make each transaction *meaningful* and *purposeful*. This doesn't mean that you carry a schedule around with you on a clipboard, and that you hit people over the head with the clipboard when they fail to meet some milestone on the schedule. It means that you act with the broad dimensions of your position in mind: to achieve production targets; to improve employee relations; to remind people to work safely; to be vigilant about equal employment opportunity, and so on. To me, there are no neutral transactions in the workplace.

As managers we set performance goals and then we manage toward the achievement of those goals. The workplace isn't a club or a spa. It is a place where intentional activity occurs to accomplish specific ends. If the working environment isn't set up to make this happen, results will reflect that fact. Let people know what you expect them to do, then make sure that they do it. If the working culture that has come to exist doesn't lend itself to this approach, then the culture needs to change.

The second dimension I would address is Planning. The tools you use to become a better planner are less important than your determination to become one. This will be a bias, but I would start by making your workplace look like planning is in evidence. Schedules are published. Meeting agendas are written and followed. Your desk is clean and neat. You return calls and remember appointments. In short, the very atmosphere in which you work looks and feels purposeful. Remember, everything in the workplace culture is an antecedent to the behaviors that people exhibit. You are a significant part of that culture.

Beyond this, I'll let you return to the book and scan through the chapters again, then fill in the chart to identify the areas you feel you need to work on. Note that in the "Dimensions" table there is a line for Other, as I know we haven't covered every management dimension. Until *Managing on Purpose II* appears, you will need to identify additional dimensions of your job on your own!

Bless you, and good managing to you.

ABOUT THE AUTHOR

Jim Hall has been a manager and a student of management for much of his professional life. His own management roles have included Father, Teacher, Department Chair, Project Manager, Editor, Technical Training Supervisor, Director of Training and Organizational Development, Knowledge Manager, Human Resources Manager, and President/General Manager. He currently does management and business consulting through Jim Hall & Associates LLC, a firm he began in 2006, in Hanover, Pennsylvania. He designs and delivers workshops and seminars and assists clients with business and strategic planning. His Human Resources certifications include PHR in 1996 and SPHR (Senior Professional in Human Resources) in 2007.

Jim Hall formed his ideas about effective management from years spent working with first line supervisors and department managers, many of whom were placed in their positions with little purposeful preparation. His ideas about how to help them have been further refined by working with business owners and managers on business and strategic planning—helping them discover where they are in their organizations, where they want to go, and determining how best to get there.

The chapters of *Managing on Purpose* are available in a variety of training packages. If you are interested in having Jim Hall tailor the lessons of the book for your organization, contact him at 717-630-0712, or email him at jimhall_503@comcast.net. You may also visit his website at www.jimhallandassociates.com or contact him through LinkedIn.

Made in the USA
Charleston, SC
19 January 2012